MY AN(
WERE C

by Sharon Sillers Floate

SOCIETY OF GENEALOGISTS ENTERPRISES LTD

Published by
Society of Genealogists Enterprises Limited
14 Charterhouse Buildings
Goswell Road
London EC1M 7BA

Third Edition © Sharon Sillers Floate 2010

ISBN: 978-1-859514-01-6

British Library Cataloguing in Publication Data
A CIP Catalogue record for this book is available from the British Library

The Society of Genealogists Enterprises Limited is a wholly owned subsidiary of the Society of Genealogists, a registered charity, no 233701

Dedication

In memory of all those ancestors who have travelled this road before me.

About the Author

Sharon Floate has been specialising in Gypsy family history since 1992 when, as a student on the Diploma of Genealogy and History of the Family course at the University of London, she began an intensive study of the lives of her East Anglian Gypsy Smiths as the subject of a thesis.

Since discovering that her five times great-grandfather Ambrose Smith and his son, also Ambrose, were transported to Australia in 1789 and 1827, she has made a special study of Gypsies who were caught up by the English legal system and writes both on this subject and on Gypsy family history. In 1994 she became a founder member of The Romany and Traveller Family History Society and continues to serve on the Society's Committee. By profession, she is a copywriter and journalist.

Cover illustration - T. B. Latchmore photograph of Sammy Draper, a well-known Gypsy musician from Hertfordshire (died 1870 in St Albans, aged 80). With kind permission of Hitchin Museum and Art Gallery.

CONTENTS

ILLUSTRATIONS

1. The marriage certificate of Edward Boswell and Siena Draper, 1846.

2. An 1871 census return showing Gypsies enumerated by nicknames.

3. A poster used in Oxford in 1871 by the 'Epping Forest Gipsies' to advertise the dances they held.

4. Typical living accommodation: a bender tent in the New Forest at the beginning of the twentieth century.

5. The baptismal entry for Plato Buckley at Wing, Buckinghamshire, 1772, recording his birth in the open air.

6. A census return for Old Buckenham, Norfolk, 1851, showing Table B and the corresponding entry for Gypsy families at the end of the enumeration district book.

7. A grant of letters of administration for the estate of William West, 1913.

8. The pedlar's certificate of Percy Shaw, 1935.

9. The settlement examination of Bartholomew Bosswell and three of his children from Kesteven Quarter Sessions, Lincolnshire, Epiphany 1797.

10. 'Borrow's Gypsies': the family tree of the East Anglian Smith family published in the *Journal of the Gypsy Lore Society*, 1910.

11. A manuscript family tree for the Draper family, discovered in a letter written by T W Thompson to fellow-Gypsiologist Otto Winstedt in 1921.

Acknowledgments

My acknowledgments are due to a large number of people whose generous help and support have helped this work come to fruition.

Of these, my special gratitude must go to Stella Colwell who first suggested that a guide to Gypsy family history would be a fitting addition to the Society's *My ancestors were...* series.

I would also like to thank my many friends in The Romany and Traveller Family History Society for their shared passion and enthusiasm for Gypsy family history, Frank Lee for his important contribution to the project, and Dr Maureen Watry, Paddy Collis and Julie Allinson of The Gypsy Collections, University of Liverpool, for their friendly help and advice over many years.

Finally, a particularly fond 'thank you' to Brian Heppell who, even though he has no Gypsy ancestors himself, takes great pleasure in accompanying me in my 'Gypsying'.

FOREWORD

Foreword to the 3rd Edition

It is now 11 years since this book first appeared. In that original edition I wrote of my hopes that in time, with the concerted help of an army of enthusiasts, it might eventually be possible to collect every reference to every Gypsy who has ever appeared in a historical document in England and Wales.

We are not there yet - but look how far we have come in that decade or so. There are three main catalysts behind the progress. Firstly, family historians who once thought that Gypsy ancestors would be virtually untraceable have instead discovered that there is a huge amount of information and resources available to them. They have taken up the search with relish and - importantly - take pleasure in sharing their finds with others.

Secondly, the Internet is now firmly established as *the* medium of choice for storing, gathering and exchanging family history information. It has been embraced by public archives, libraries, commercial bodies and private individuals alike, making their catalogues, documents, complete books, family trees and personal histories widely available to all and - through this - often connecting 'cousins' with the same ancestral Gypsy lines. And with the arrival of faster broadband speeds - and the growth in the phenomena of social networking and digital photography - it is now feasible and cost effective for researchers to share online not only their written documents but also their visual heritage by uploading albums of family photographs, old films and videos: a rich resource that makes history come alive.

Thirdly, there are the many indexing initiatives that are working their way through classes of documents we would once have considered too large or too daunting to tackle alone. We give hardly a second thought now to the miracle that has put millions of census records at our fingertips online to reveal our Gypsy ancestors in seconds. Now the indexers are addressing even bigger challenges on our behalf. One example is the plan by the Metropolitan Archives to digitise their complete holdings - from parish registers to Poor Law records - and make them available online: a move that opens up the lives of London's many Gypsy communities to us.

Finally, I would again like to thank all those who welcomed the first two editions of this book and who - I hope as a result - have been inspired to take up the baton and research and preserve the history of their own Gypsy ancestors and heritage. But there is still room - and scope - for many more pioneers. Over to you!

Sharon Sillers Floate
August 2010

Foreword to the 1st Edition 1999

There is a long-standing belief in family history circles that if you ever discover you have Gypsy ancestry you may as well abandon your search immediately. Certainly it has often deterred even the most determined genealogist - myself included.

I came across the first clue that I had Gypsy blood in the early 1980s, soon after I had become caught up by the passion that is family history. The marriage certificate of my great-great grandmother gave her name as 'Lementeni Smith', daughter of William Smith, a horsedealer. The combination of an unusual forename, a traditional Gypsy surname and a typical Gypsy occupation (plus the hint of a family legend) suggested there was no doubt about it. Lementeni and her family were also noticeable by their absence in conventional family history sources such as the GRO and census records, trade directories and the registers of the parish of marriage and contiguous parishes.

Being a novice genealogist at the time and disappointed at not being able to make any progress whatsoever in the search for Lementeni and her antecedents, I reluctantly put the Smith file on one side and turned my attention to my 'settled' ancestors, imagining (in my innocence) that they were going to be far easier to find.

It was over 10 years before I took up that file again. Now more experienced in genealogy and faced with the prospect of choosing a suitable subject for a thesis as part of the University of London's Diploma course in Genealogy and the History of the Family, my Gypsies seemed the ideal challenge. I was particularly attracted by the fact that Gypsy family history remained an area of genealogy that was still largely unknown and untouched by others and so offered room for some pioneering work. It still does!

By this time I had made contact with a small number of experts in the history of the Gypsies. Armed with their suggestions of key texts to look at, I headed for the British Library for the first time. It was an eye-opener in more ways than one. In the first book I called up - a copy of the *Journal of the Gypsy Lore Society* of 1910 - the pages opened at a family tree for the Smiths. Attached to one of the branches was my Lementeni: the one and only time in my career as a family historian that I have ever had the gratification of being handed my family tree on a plate. But this was only the beginning.

After all those years of thinking that the lives of our Gypsy ancestors had gone unnoticed and unrecorded, I quickly discovered that quite the reverse was true. It seemed that in the nineteenth century, while some ethnographers and anthropologists were travelling the world in search of exotic peoples, others had discovered a fit subject for observation and documentation far closer to home: the Romani Gypsies of Britain. Their records often include detailed genealogies and have been left to us in a number of forms. The *Journal of the Gypsy Lore Society* is the pre-eminent source but as important are the massive collections of manuscripts and notebooks compiled by these 'Gypsiologists' of the nineteenth and early twentieth centuries, their non-fiction printed works, semi-autobiographical novels, drawings, paintings and photographs.

A second key advantage in Gypsy research is - by paradox - the illiteracy of the Gypsies of the past. In a community where the majority were unable to read or write, greater than usual emphasis was placed on the value of oral history. So in interviewing Gypsies of the nineteenth and early twentieth centuries, Gypsiologists were able to record genealogies, customs, language use and folklore that dated back many generations - and sometimes many centuries - preserved and passed down as a treasured heritage. The result is a database of family information that is rarely available when researching non-Gypsy families at the same social level at the same period.

Consciously or unconsciously - and no doubt in spite of their best endeavours - the Gypsy people have left a trail of clues throughout their long history in Britain. This guide is intended to show you how to read, interpret and follow those clues and so track down those most elusive of ancestors.

The scope of this guide

The people we know as Gypsies first arrived in Britain at the end of the fifteenth or the beginning of the sixteenth century.

However, in the belief that most family historians will be interested in working back from a more recent date, this guide concentrates on useful sources for genealogical material dating from the eighteenth to the twentieth centuries.

It has also been essential to set some geographical parameters. The information that follows largely concerns English and Welsh Gypsies - the 'Romanichals' as they call themselves in their own language, Romani. Readers with Gypsy ancestors in Scotland and Ireland can nevertheless take a great deal of what follows as relevant to their own research strategy and are particularly encouraged to read the section on p.69 on the *Journal of the Gypsy Lore Society* as this has included many articles on the history, customs and genealogies of Gypsies of those and other countries of the world.

CHAPTER ONE
Historical introduction

T he people we know today as Gypsies are generally believed to have originated about a thousand years ago in Rajasthan in North West India. There continues to be debate among historians as to the reasons why they left their homeland and ventured west. One view is that they were refugees escaping a war or famine. Another that they were captured as slaves and taken to Persia. Another that they were recruited as mercenaries to join a foreign army. And yet another that they were already nomads and simply decided to cross the Indus to find fortune on the other side.

It is also not known whether their westward migration happened once or several times in the next few hundred years, with people going backwards and forwards between India and the countries of modern-day Europe. Some of the migrants stopped part-way - hence the Gypsy communities found today in the countries of Central Europe such as Albania, Hungary and Romania.

Others continued as far west as France, where Gypsies are first recorded in 1419, and then into Spain and Portugal.[1] It was from France, at a point in the late 1400s or the first few years of the sixteenth century, that a group of

Gypsies followed the trade routes from Continental Europe across to the British Isles.

Here the first documented sighting of them was in Scotland in 1505 in an account of the High Treasurer.[2] This recorded the fact that at the command of King James IV a sum of £7 had been given to a group of *'Egiptianis'*: a huge amount at a time when £1 might represent a year's wages. The fact that the High Treasurer did not see it necessary to explain what an *'Egiptiani'* was could be taken as evidence that the Gypsies had already been in Scotland for some time before this date.

In England the earliest mention of Gypsies so far discovered is in the time of Henry VIII in a work entitled *A Dialogue of Sir Thomas More, Knight*.[3] In this More recalls that at an inquest he attended in 1514 into the death of Richard Hunne in the Lollards' Tower, one of the witnesses was referred to as an *'Egyptian'* woman who had lodged in Lambeth and was renowned for her ability to read palms.

The movement of Gypsies across England and into Wales obviously took a little longer. It is not until 1579 that the first mention is made of Gypsies in a Welsh document in the Acts of the Privy Council. This records that on 10 January of that year (Old Style) the Sheriff of Radnorshire apprehended *'40 vagrant persons terming themselves Egiptiens'*[4].

In all these cases, for 'Egyptians' read 'Gypsies'*. This was the term used to describe them in documents in the British Isles from the sixteenth century until at least the first quarter of the eighteenth century. The popular belief of the time was that they belonged to a tribe of people who had originated in Little Egypt. Their dark skins, exotic oriental-style clothes, strange Arabic-sounding language and alien customs no doubt reinforced this very strongly. The Gypsies did nothing to disabuse the people they met of their mistake, finding there was often a financial advantage in arousing curiosity and maintaining the mystery of their origins.

There is much evidence that despite the widespread xenophobia and superstitious beliefs of earlier centuries, the Gypsies were at first generally welcomed or at least tolerated. Then, as in our own times, they provided valuable craft skills, particularly in the working of metal. They were willing and able repair-men, capable of turning their hands to fixing almost anything. For the isolated rural communities of England and Wales, they also brought with them essential items of basketware, cooking

---

* As the word 'Gypsy' derives from 'Egyptian', it is the modern accepted convention to spell it with a 'y'. As it also represents a member of a recognised ethnic group, it should also always be spelt with a capital letter.

utensils, haberdashery and the like which were frequently not available from any other convenient source.

For the farmers, they provided horses. On feast days and at fairs and weddings, they entertained with music and dance. The women also seemed to have the mystic ability to foretell the future, although this trade carried with it the risk of being accused of witchcraft and punished accordingly.

In whatever country they settled in their westward migration from India, there was always a distance between the Gypsies and the non-Gypsies: the *'gaujos'*, as the Gypsies call them. This separation may have been imposed by the non-Gypsies but the Gypsies were happy to maintain it, in the same way that other immigrant groups have tended to want to protect and preserve their own customs, culture, beliefs and language in the midst of a foreign host society. The Gypsies perceived the alien lifestyle and lack of morals of the native English and Welsh people as a cultural threat to them and their children.

The decision of the Gypsies to remain as outsiders to the settled society - apart from the necessary process of trade with *gaujos* - was also a form of protection against persecution and prosecution. For in the majority of the countries they passed through, their passage soon resulted in severe anti-Gypsy legislation.

This was the pattern in the British Isles too. It was not long before the guarded welcome or toleration originally extended to them on their arrival was replaced by a long series of laws and proclamations designed to banish, punish, reform or exterminate Gypsies because of what was seen as their outlandish, deviant behaviour, contrary to the established norms of society.

The first English Act in which Gypsies were formally named was the 'Egyptians Act' of 1530. This had a dual purpose: firstly, to prevent the immigration of Gypsies into England from the Continent and secondly, to exile those who were already in the country. The latter were threatened with imprisonment and having to forfeit all their possessions if they did not leave England within 16 days of the proclamation.

In 1554 the Egyptians Act was reinforced with a measure which made the simple fact of being a Gypsy a capital crime. As well as being forbidden to enter England, those who were already in the country were liable to be arrested and executed. This legislation remarkably remained on the Statute Book until 1783, meaning that anyone born a Gypsy during the intervening time was constantly under risk of death.

In 1562 in an England still troubled by Gypsies, the penalties of both of the previous Egyptians Acts were extended to include what were termed *'counterfeit Egyptians'*. By this the law meant people from the settled society who had joined bands of Gypsies or who travelled and lived as though they were Gypsies. From our modern-day perspective it is difficult to understand why anyone who had a choice would elect to join a group of people who were under capital sentence. The 1562 Act stated that counterfeit Gypsies should be considered felons - that is, in the same category as someone who had committed a major crime - and *'suffer Paynes of Death, Losse of Landes and Goodes as in cases of Felonye'*.

The Egyptians Acts of the sixteenth century were difficult to enforce and relatively ineffective in controlling the Gypsy population - as is evident in the estimate that during the reign of Elizabeth I (1533-1603) there were about 10,000 Gypsies in England and Wales, perhaps proving the old Gypsy proverb:

> *'If you cut a Gypsy into 10 pieces you will not have killed him but you will have made 10 Gypsies.'*[5]

In 1598 the English Parliament took a different tack and passed a bill entitled *'An Acte for the Punyshment of Rogues, Vagabonds and Sturdy Beggars'*. This gave Justices of the Peace the right to banish people they believed came into these categories to 'such parts beyond the seas' as were designated by the Privy Council. The authorities believed banishment was a cheaper, safer and more certain way of punishing people than by imprisoning them.

Into the category of *'rogues, vagabonds and sturdy beggars'* came anyone who was considered to be *'dangerous to the inferior sort of people'* or *'such as will not be reformed of their roguish way of life'*. This naturally encompassed Gypsies too because travelling was fundamental to their culture and way of life and not something they would be willing or able to forego even under duress.

In 1662 the Settlement Act formalised previous provisions for the treatment of vagrants and again made it possible for Justices of the Peace to cause any *'rogue, vagabond or sturdy beggar to be convicted, adjudged incorrigible and transported'*, again without having any other charges against them. This Act provided a restraining influence not only on Gypsies but on every member of the population, preventing most people from travelling at will if they did not carry appropriate documentation or sufficient personal funds with them. As the previous Egyptians Acts were still in force, the Gypsy was now doubly liable to be prosecuted for his travelling lifestyle.

The litany of legislation and proclamations against Gypsies and the antagonism against them from settled society continued in this vein for the next three centuries, as the long calendar of Acts affecting them shows. This is given in Appendix 1 on p.91 and includes both legislation which was specifically designed to control Gypsies as a discrete group and legislation which affected the whole population but which had a particular impact on Gypsies because of the differences between their lifestyle and customs and those of the *gaujos*.

There are a number of important implications for family historians as a result of the treatment the Gypsies have received from non-Gypsies in Britain:

• As outcasts of settled society, Gypsies usually attempted to limit their dealings with officialdom to the very minimum. This means they would consciously avoid such responsibilities as census enumeration and post-1837 civil registration.

• The lack of trust between Gypsies and non-Gypsies means that when Gypsies were forced to provide personal details they might suspect the motives of the authorities and so conceal information or provide inaccurate information.

• The amount of legislation which had a direct effect on Gypsies' everyday lives means they were more likely than the average *gaujo* to appear in legal and settlement records.

• The Gypsies have a fierce pride in their own culture and customs and throughout history have wished to protect and preserve them both from observation and contamination by outsiders: a secret society as it were. Most of the writings about the social and cultural history of the Gypsies in England and Wales have been by non-Gypsies. Such accounts will be rather what the Gypsies were prepared to reveal to a *gaujo* or embroidered versions of the truth - what the Gypsy believed the non-Gypsy wanted to hear. The *gaujo*'s misunderstanding of the true nature of events witnessed might also lead to misinterpretations. It is important to remember this element of secrecy, particularly when consulting Gypsy genealogies which have been gathered as oral history by non-Gypsies.

For books giving an account of the Gypsies' journey from India to the west and their history in Britain, see the Bibliography on p.97 and Background reading on p.101.

CHAPTER TWO

Gypsy or non-Gypsy? The clues to identity

O ne of the delights of family history is hunting down the evidence which proves that the family legend holds a nugget of truth.

If all you have is the name of an ancestor and the hint of a family tradition of 'Gypsy blood' to go on, how are you to tell if he or she might be a Gypsy? There are a number of clues to look for before you start your search. According to the modern-day expert on Gypsies, David Smith, to be one hundred percent confident of an individual's Gypsy origins, you should seek evidence of all four of the following in the same individual:

1. Traditional Gypsy surname

Your ancestor may carry one of the traditional Gypsy surnames. Boswell, Cooper, Smith and Lee are a few of the better-known ones but it has to be remembered that these names are also very common among the non-Gypsy population.

There are however literally hundreds of other surnames which although less familiar are equally authentic and carry a long pedigree of use by

Gypsy families. See Appendix 2 for a select list of examples. A more comprehensive directory can be found in Robert Dawson's *Gypsy Names for Genealogists Volume 1: Surnames.*

Some surnames are closely connected with particular regions of England and Wales. As typical examples: Doe is a Gypsy surname found in Hampshire; Gaskin is generally found in eastern England between Yorkshire and Suffolk; Lock is often an alias used by members of the Boswell family in North Wales. Discovering an ancestor with one of these names in the 'correct' region would strengthen the case for their being a Gypsy.

2. Unusual forename

One of the key identifiers of a Gypsy is an unusual forename. This is not to say that Gypsy parents never named their child John Smith or Mary Lee. But alongside children with conventional names you are likely to find siblings who have been baptised with exuberant, highly imaginative forenames that could range from Arkless to Sanspirella and from Prettymaid (male) to Zephyrus. For the most part they are names that would rarely if ever be found in the non-Gypsy population in the same time period. There are more examples on p.15/16 - as there are in Robert Dawson's *Gypsy Names for Genealogists Volume 2: Forenames.*

3. Typical Gypsy occupation

Another important marker of Gypsy identity is occupation. For the most part Gypsies were involved in 'service industries' - trades or crafts that they could easily conduct and carry with them on the road and supply on demand to customers. The most common ones you are likely to encounter in records include:

Tinker or Tinsmith	Dealer	Caneworker
Brazier	Horsedealer	Chairbottomer
Grinder, knife-grinder	Cutler	Chimney sweep
or scissor-grinder	Basketmaker	Hawker

Where the authorities have not felt it necessary to record occupation as such - for example, in the space allowed for occupations in post-1813 baptismal registers - you might instead find an attempt at a description of the status of an individual, as the writer saw it. The word 'Gypsy' may be included here (spelt in a variety of ways) as may 'vagrant', 'traveller', 'stroller' or 'stranger'.

CERTIFIED COPY OF AN ENTRY OF MARRIAGE

GIVEN AT THE GENERAL REGISTER OFFICE

Application Number WOO3832

1846. Marriage solemnized at *St Nicholas Church* in the *Parish* of *Liverpool* in the County of *Lancaster*

No.	When Married	Name and Surname	Age	Condition	Rank or Profession	Residence at the Time of Marriage	Father's Name and Surname	Rank or Profession of Father
277	15th November 1846	Edward Boswell	full	Bachelor	Labourer	Upper Milk Street	Moses Boswell	Cutler
		Siena Draper	minor		Spinster	Upper Milk Street	Israel Draper	Basket Maker

Married in the *Church of St Nicholas* according to the Rites and Ceremonies of the Established Church, *after Banns* by me.

This Marriage was solemnized between us,	Edward Boswell his X Mark	In the Presence of us,	Isaac Gibson his X Mark	Abel L Lamb 110 Cavcat...
	Siena Draper her X Mark		Elizabeth Garthouse her X Mark	

Liverpool Febuary 1993

... day of ... 5th

MX 618292

CERTIFIED to be a true copy of an entry in the certified copy of a register of Marriage in the Registration District of ...
Given at the General Register Office, under the Seal of the said Office, the ...

This certificate is issued in pursuance of section 65 of the Marriage Act 1949. Sub-section 3 of that section provides that any certified copy of an entry purporting to be sealed or stamped with the seal of the General Register Office shall be received as evidence of the marriage to which it relates without any further or other proof of the entry, and no certified copy purporting to have been given in the said Office shall be of any force or effect unless it is sealed or stamped as aforesaid.

CAUTION.—It is an offence to falsify a certificate or to make or knowingly use a false certificate or a copy of a false certificate intending it to be accepted as genuine to the prejudice of any person, or to possess a certificate knowing it to be false without lawful authority.

WARNING: THIS CERTIFICATE IS NOT EVIDENCE OF THE IDENTITY OF THE PERSON PRESENTING IT.

Form A(HMX)

1. The marriage certificate of Edward Boswell and Siena Draper, married at St Nicholas, Liverpool, in November 1846 while their families were overwintering in the city (Crown copyright. Published by permission of the Controller of HMSO and the Office for National Statistics).

9

4. Evidence of mobility

Nomadism was the way of life for a Gypsy. To confirm identity you therefore need to seek evidence that your ancestor travelled. As examples, you might gain this from a census return which shows that almost every child in the same family has a different place of birth; from a settlement examination and removal order; or from a post-1813 baptismal register which gives 'of no fixed place of abode' under the abode heading.

The marriage certificate on p.9 provides hard evidence of three of the necessary 'coincidents' in the major individuals involved:

• Traditional Gypsy surnames - Draper and Boswell
• Unusual forenames - Tiso, Siena and Israel
• Typical occupations - cutler and basketmaker

A marriage certificate rarely shows evidence of mobility. In the case of these individuals this comes from additional research which shows that the bride was baptised in Doddington, Northamptonshire, in 1822 and her father in Therfield, Hertfordshire, in 1786; the groom was baptised in Collingham, Yorkshire, in 1815 and his father in Epping, Essex, in 1778. The wedding took place in St Nicholas, Liverpool, in November 1846 when the two families were undoubtedly overwintering in the poor, working-class Scotland Road area of that city.

With evidence as clear as this, you need have no doubts about your ancestors being Gypsies - and in the following pages, you will discover how to gather such evidence not only by taking a different approach to conventional family history sources but also by discovering the huge body of information that is available on Gypsy families in specialist sources.

CHAPTER THREE

*The social organisation and customs of
the Gypsy and their impact on family
history research*

There are a number of key differences between the social organisation,
culture and customs of Gypsies and non-Gypsies which need to be
taken into consideration when researching a Gypsy family tree.

A matrilineal and matrilocal society

Gypsies are one of the few racial groups or societies in history to have
practised 'matriliny' and 'matrilocality'. These are terms used by
anthropologists to describe a society where men would join their wife's
family on marriage or when a permanent relationship was formed and
where the children of that marriage or relationship would remain with their
maternal relatives on the death of the mother. As a widower, the father
would generally return to his own family group until such a time as he
married again when he would join his new wife's group. Family groups
would sometimes be headed by a matriarchal figure.[6]

There is much evidence to suggest that this was the practice of many
Gypsy families in England and Wales in the eighteenth and nineteenth
centuries - and for the family historian its implications are as follows:

11

- There was no compulsion for a child to take the surname of its father or a wife her husband's surname on marriage. A husband could in fact take his wife's surname. Individuals may therefore be found using both names interchangeably.

- Children who lose their mother may be found living with her relatives, being cared for by their maternal grandparents or their mother's siblings, rather than returning with their father to his own tribe and their paternal relatives.

- Such children may decide to discard their father's surname and permanently use their mother's surname.

- They may also refer to their maternal grandparents as their parents if they have been raised by them. This could affect the name given as 'father' on marriage certificates.

- Children whose mother remarried might occasionally use the surname of their stepfather as one of the names available to them.

- You may find travelling groups containing an apparently disparate collection of surnames. A deeper investigation may reveal that all its members are related through their maternal line.

Choice of 'marriage' partners

"Lees recordin' to rights should marry with Lees' said Ira Lee to me once."

So begins Chapter IV of Vesey-Fitzgerald's *Gypsies of Britain* concerning the customs relating to Gypsy marriage - or more usually the customs which accompanied the formation of a permanent relationship, not necessarily formalised by a church or register office ceremony.[7]

Vesey-Fitzgerald goes on to report that in-marriage - restricting one's choice of partner to someone of the same surname - was a common practice among members of some of the major English Gypsy families of the past including the Smiths, Grays and Herons. And certainly there is hard evidence of this in the genealogies collected by the Gypsiologists.

It is easy to understand why these restrictions existed and why marriage with a member of the same family or travelling group was preferred for both sexes.

There is a popular stereotype of Gypsy women as sensual beings, unfettered by the conventions and moralities of non-Gypsy society. It therefore comes as a surprise to many people to learn that strict moral codes governed the lives of young unmarried Gypsy women, far stricter than those determining the accepted behaviour of non-Gypsy women. Often the only men that a young woman would come into contact with socially would be her near-relatives in the same travelling group. This meant that marriages or partnerships between cousins were common and in some cases the only option. Such a liaison would of course mean that the man would be able to stay with the same group under the conventions of matrilocality, thus avoiding a break of both emotional and economic ties.

Where a friendship or cousinship did become more serious, the young woman would generally be chaperoned in all her meetings with her young man and there would be no intimacy between them until the marriage ceremony had been performed, either formally in a church or register office or by a Gypsy ceremony. It may be useful to note when searching for an official marriage that according to Vesey-Fitzgerald Gypsy men and women married at a considerably younger age than their counterparts in the settled population, women being 19-20 and men 21-22.[8]

'Serial' partnerships

Given the regulation of the social interaction between Gypsy men and women, it might seem curious to learn that many Gypsies of both sexes indulged in 'serial partnerships', perhaps having relationships and having children by two or three people in the course of their lives without the need for death or divorce to put a formal end to each partnership.

There are also documented cases of polygamy, perhaps reflecting the Gypsies' oriental origins. Gypsy men might have more than one partner at the same time, including sometimes wives who were sisters, each one having her own accommodation for her own children.[9] This will then explain why you may find baptisms of a series of children in the course of a few years where the father is the same but the mother's name is apparently different. This should not be taken to mean that a previous spouse has died. However, you also need to keep in mind that the name change may be a whim on the part of the mother in dealing with the Church authorities or a case of the vicar mishearing an unconventional forename.

Marrying out

There have of course been Gypsy marriages with non-Gypsies throughout history. Gypsy men marrying non-Gypsy women would generally expect their wives to join their family group and live by the codes which govern Gypsy life.

For Gypsy women who married out, there could be two courses of action. The new *gaujo* husband might expect his wife to join him in settled society, to live in a house and to raise their children as non-Gypsies, so breaking familial ties and losing their cultural identity.

Occasionally a Gypsy group would allow a male non-Gypsy outsider to join them, provided that he was prepared to live and work as they did. This often explains the appearance in a Gypsy community of a non-Gypsy surname which subsequent children may carry and which then over time comes to be accepted as a 'true' Gypsy name.

Extended family groups

Gypsies travelled in extended family groups, with siblings, cousins and older generations sometimes all moving together. Different families which were related by marriage might also travel and/or live closely together. This means that if you are researching East Anglian Smiths - who had close ties with the Boswells and Robinsons over many generations - it is a good idea to look out for these latter names too in your research. Their existence in a document or record may point to the fact that there were Smiths in the same locality at the same time.

Naming customs

Choice of surnames
When the Gypsies first arrived in Britain they naturally brought with them their own foreign surnames. A writ signed by James V of Scotland in 1540 records a group under the leadership of John Faw, described as 'Lord and Earl of Little Egypt', whose names include Anteane Donea, Satona Fingo, Nona Finco, Towla Bailzon and Demeo Matskalla.[10] Whether these bear any resemblance to the individuals' real names or were simply a clerk's best attempt at writing down what he thought he heard will probably never be known.

In order to achieve a degree of assimilation into their host society - at least enough to remove barriers to trade - these early Gypsies either anglicised the names they already carried or adopted local surnames. 'Smith' for example is a translation of *'Petulengro'* which means 'horseshoe maker' in Romani. Other families took their pick of the names they heard about them. Often they astutely chose surnames which carried a high status such as those belonging to great estate owners. Stanley and Lovell are two such examples.

It is important to keep in mind that some of the accepted 'traditional Gypsy names' (as listed in Appendix 2 and in Robert Dawson's *Gypsy Names for Genealogists Volume I: Surnames*) are common among non-Gypsies. This can make it difficult to determine if the 'John Boswell' or the 'Mary Lovell' you discover in a census return or baptismal register is a Gypsy or not. Supporting information should always be sought from such evidence as occupation and distance from birthplace before coming to conclusions.

Choice of forenames

As explained earlier in the section on determining Gypsy identity, one of the key identifiers in searching for Gypsies is their choice of unusual forenames for their children. This is a custom which continues to the present day.

To give an idea of the scope of such names, here is a small selection gathered from original documents of the past three centuries. Some are often used in an abbreviated form and these are given in brackets where appropriate:

Female names

Alamina (Mina)	Erosabella	Pizinnia
Aquilla	Fambridge (Femi)	Queenation
Athalia	Kerelenda	Richenda
Azubia (Zuby)	Lementeni (Teni)	Shurensi (Shuri)
Britannia	Levaithan	Silberania
Cinderella (Relly)	Maresko	Sinfi
Cinnaminta (Minti)	Marella (Relly)	Tranetta
Desibera	Ocean	Trenit
Dorelia	Parthena	

Male names

Adolphus	Kisby	Rodolphus
Alibon	Lacy	Riley
Alma	Lomas/Lumas	Saunders
Bendigo	Mackenzie (Kenza)	Sharpisis
Bohemius	Major	Shipton
Dangerfield	Mendoza	Solivano
Diverus	Napoleon (Poley)	Silvester
Frampton	Pender	Tyso/Taiso/Tiso
Joiner	Righteous	

Taken as a whole, such a variety of names may appear to show little pattern or obvious meaning. There are however a number of common threads running through Gypsy naming customs, some of which can hold useful clues for the family historian. These include:

• Children might be named after their place of birth: for example, 'Shipton' may come from one of the Shipton villages in Oxfordshire; 'Fambridge' may relate to one of two villages of that name in Essex.

• By extension this might also include landmarks in the vicinity of the birth: for example, Evergreen or Reservoir.

• Surnames were used as forenames - as was sometimes the practice among non-Gypsies who wanted to preserve an important surname in the maternal line. Gypsy examples include Mackenzie and Saunders.

• Commemoration of historical events or important figures in history: Trafalgar, Crimea, Wellington and Plato. If the event was recent history, it may point to the approximate birth year of the individual concerned. For example, Alma Boswell (male) was born in 1855, the year after the Crimean War battle of the same name.

• 'Ancient' names which were common in non-Gypsy society in earlier centuries. These preserved names - such as Hamelen or Oti - may date from the Norman or medieval period and therefore sound strange to our ears.

• The rarer biblical names or names once favoured by the Puritans: Noah, Methuselah, Delilah, Constance, Comfort, Liberty (male), Trinity and Repentance.

- Names which sound attractive, no matter what their real sense in English. Two frequently quoted examples of this are 'Aluminium' and 'Scarlatina'.

- The appearance of the same unusual name in two different families usually indicates a link between them, rather than a strange coincidence.[11]

A number of points relating to the use of forenames need to be considered in your research:

- *Mishearing and misinterpretation by the authorities*
  This is a caveat that practised family historians will already be aware of. It is clear from the transcriptions of the speech of Gypsies of the nineteenth and early twentieth centuries (such as those recorded in the *Journal of the Gypsy Lore Society* - see p.69) that many spoke English in an accented way. Few were able to read or write. This means that when they gave their name or the name of the child to the census enumerator or the vicar performing a baptism, it could easily be wrongly recorded. Non-Gypsies undoubtedly suffered in a similar way if they spoke with a regional accent or had a speech impediment. There was however a greater risk of a Gypsy forename being misspelt because it was often likely that the hearer had never encountered it before.

- *Abbreviations*
  Some Gypsies may have been given more conventional names - but there was a tendency to abbreviate these in a way that is not immediately obvious to the non-Gypsy population. Elisha for example might become 'Lusha'; Lydia might become 'Liti'; Herbert might become 'Rabi'. These truncated versions might then be offered up in the place of full names or used to baptise subsequent generations of children in the short form rather than the full form.

- *Nicknames or bye-names*
  Like non-Gypsies, Gypsies would often name their children after members of their own family or after members of a family they had close links with and perhaps travelled with. This custom often resulted in two or more individuals in the same travelling group having exactly the same forename and surname. In this instance bye-names were frequently used as identifiers: for example, a diminutive - Johna; a descriptive - Little John; or a nickname - Longsnout John.[12] There could be occasions where these names rather than baptismal names were offered up to the authorities for inclusion in a parish register or census return.

For a comprehensive list of forenames, see Robert Dawson's *Gypsy names for Genealogists Volume 2: Forenames.*

or rough of	Municipal Ward of	Parliamentary Bo
ea	Attercliffe	Sheffiel

SES Unin-habited (U.) or Building (B.)	NAME and Surname of each Person	RELATION to Head of Family	C DI
	alias Francis Brown Henry Stapleton	Head	
	Black Bud	Son	
	Cox	Son	
	alias misty Brown Granney	Mistress	
	Fancy	Daur	
	Frightful	Son	
	Black Sandy	Son	
	Nipper *Kentuck Harriet Brown*	Daur	
	William Gray	Head	
	Mary Do	Wife	
	Sarah Do	Daur	
	Richard Do	Son	
	John Do	Son	
	Annie Do	Daur	
	Snowelly Do	Daur	
	Emjelina Do	Daur	
	Clementa Do	Daur	

2. An 1871 census return for Attercliffe, Yorkshire, showing Gypsies enumerated by nicknames (Crown copyright material in The National Archives, reproduced by permission of the Controller of HMSO. Ref. RG10 4698 folio 62).

Occupations

As explained earlier, occupation is another of the key identifiers in determining if an individual was a Gypsy or non-Gypsy.

Itinerancy as a way of life obviously had an important influence in determining the kind of work Gypsies could take up. Their independence and their reluctance to become too closely involved with non-Gypsies meant that very few took up permanent fixed employment in the waged labour market until such a time as they became settled or moved into a house. It is generally only from the middle of the nineteenth century that you begin to find some Gypsies described as 'labourers'.

For the most part, the Gypsies' occupations revolved around what we today term 'service industries'.[13] They travelled to their customers, providing valuable craft and repair skills, entertainment and goods for sale: services which in the largely rural England and Wales of the years before industrialisation were rarely available to customers from any other source apart from craftsmen in large towns and the occasional passing pedlar. These occupations can be categorised under five main headings:

• The sale of goods made by the Gypsies themselves and largely their monopoly: pegs, basketware, mats, meat skewers, straw beehives, brooms, brushes and sieves.

• The sale of goods purchased from wholesalers: horses, pots, pans and haberdashery.

• The provision of repair skills: tinkering, knife and scissor-grinding, umbrella repairing and chairbottoming.

• The provision of entertainment: playing musical instruments at fairs and weddings, fortune-telling, holding dances, providing or managing fairground rides and boxing booths.

• The provision of seasonal agricultural labour on a casual basis: particularly at times of high demand such as sowing and harvest. Gypsies - the women above all - are closely associated with fruit, hop and flower picking.

When these are then translated for entry in a parish register or a census return, the typical occupations you need to look out for under these categories include:

The Tribe of
EPPING FOREST
GIPSIES

Intend giving a GRAND

BALL

ON FRIDAY NEXT, MARCH 24, 1871,

In the Field where they are located

IN BINSEY LANE,

A LARGE TENT beautifully illuminated will be
Erected for the occasion. The

KING AND QUEEN

WILL BE PRESENT.

And the Public will have a grand opportunity of seeing

GIPSY LIFE.

THIS TRIBE HAS CAUSED GREAT EXCITEMENT IN
THEIR TRAVELS THROUGH GREAT BRITAIN.

The Ground will be opened at FOUR o'lock until SIX,
p.m. admission, Two Shillings. From SEVEN o'clock,
One Shilling admittance

A FIRST CLASS QUADRILLE BAND WILL ATTEND.

Manager—Mr Young. Refreshments provided by Mr.
Barrett, 18, Corn Market Street. Every attention will be
paid to the comfort of the Public.

3. A poster used in Oxford in 1871 by the 'Epping Forest Gipsies' to advertise the dances they held (With kind permission of the Bodleian Library, University of Oxford. Ref. Gough Adds Fol A 139 item 34).

20

- Basketmaker, clothes peg maker or dealer, sievemaker, net maker

- Hawker, licensed hawker, pedlar, general dealer, marine stores dealer, horsedealer

- Cutler, tinker, knife-grinder, grinder, caneworker, brazier, tinman, tinsmith, chairbottomer or mender, chimney sweep, umbrella repairer

- Musician, fiddler, fortune-teller

- Harvestman or woman, hop picker, rat catcher

- Where no occupation is given, individuals may be termed 'vagrant,' 'traveller', 'vagabond', 'sojourner', 'tramper' or 'stroller'.

In contrast to most non-Gypsies, it was common for one individual to have many different occupations during his or her lifetime. This means that you may well gather up a series of baptisms of children in the course of a few years where the occupation of the father is different on each occasion.

The women in Gypsy communities had a key economic role to play. As well as being involved with the men in the production of items to sell, it was generally their exclusive responsibility to hawk these and other bought-in items. They would also frequently combine this with the offer of fortune-telling when calling door to door. This *'dukkering'* too was their exclusive domain. Few if any Gypsy men would deign to read palms, even if they knew how.

Perhaps surprisingly, in census returns you will often find that the women in a Gypsy group have occupations recorded by their names, whereas this was frequently not the case for non-Gypsy women.

Accommodation

Despite the rather romanticised view many people have of Gypsies in history roaming over the landscape in a brightly coloured caravan, the reality was very different. The van - or *'vardo'* as it is known in Romani - is a comparatively recent introduction as living accommodation for Travellers. It has only been in use since the middle of the nineteenth century and then only by the more wealthy Gypsy families.

4. Typical living accommodation: a bender tent in the New Forest at the beginning of the twentieth century, taken from a contemporary postcard

Before this 'waggon time' - as the Gypsies call it - families would shelter in 'benders'. These tents were formed by constructing a framework of flexible wooden branches (hence the name 'bender') which was then covered with old blankets, canvas or tarpaulins, fastened in place with blackthorn pins which had been treated to harden them. In the late nineteenth century, some Gypsies also used ex-Army bell tents. Some Scottish Travellers continued to use tents until the 1970s.

In the winter, Gypsies might gravitate from the countryside to the outskirts of the larger towns or cities or areas of wasteland in town or city centres where they could feel more confident of finding a constant captive market for their services and products. They would generally continue to use their traditional tents or vans but it was not unknown for some Gypsy families to overwinter in houses.

There are instances of some pitching their tents or vans on wasteground on one side of a road and living in rented accommodation on the other. These temporary communities would generally be formed in the poorer, working-class areas. If the Gypsies happened to be in the houses on census night, they would naturally be enumerated as though they were normal house-dwellers. A good local history book might point you to the streets where the cheaper lodging houses or tenements were to be found.

Looking further back in history before the time of the bender tent - in the eighteenth century and earlier - Gypsies would seek shelter in barns and outhouses, with or without permission from their owners. In some regions there were buildings that were so regularly used by Travellers and so well known in the travelling community that they acquired special names. The 'Travellers House' or 'Beggars House' in Aylesford, Kent, formally known as the Parsonage Barn, is one such example.[14]

Where there were no buildings available, the Gypsy families would simply shelter in the open air under hedges. No doubt many of our ancestors in earlier centuries first saw the light of day under a hawthorn bush, even in the depths of winter. You are therefore likely to come across entries in parish registers similar to this one:

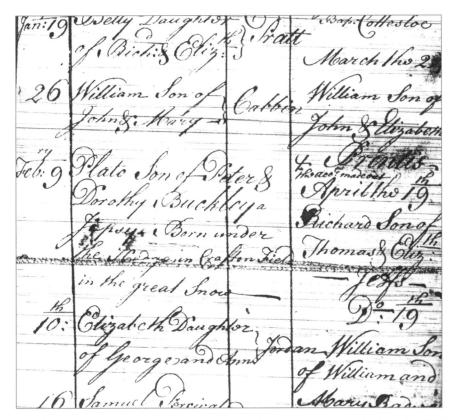

5. The February 1772 baptismal entry for Plato Buckley, a 'Jipsy born under the Hedge in Crafton Field in the great Snow' in the parish of Wing, Buckinghamshire (With kind permission of the Vicar of Wing and the Centre for Buckinghamshire Studies. Ref. PR 234/1/3).

Circuits and settlements

Contrary to popular belief, Gypsies of the past did not generally travel large distances in a haphazard way. The course of their journeys was usually well planned and repeated year after year to take advantage of the different trading opportunities offered by the annual calendar of fairs or markets in a particular region of the country.

Depending on which part of the country your ancestors looked on as their 'base', you may find that they did not venture beyond a single county. If, for example, that county offered a large number of centres of population, a year-round calendar of fairs to attend and opportunities for different kinds of agricultural employment throughout most of the year, there would be little need for the Gypsies to travel further afield.

Conversely, in a sparsely populated region with large distances between the market towns - such as East Anglia - Gypsies often had to travel extensively, crossing and re-crossing county borders in the course of their annual itinerary.

With the help of a census return showing the birthplaces of children, combined with a calendar of fairs, it may be possible to plot the course of a family's travels. This could in turn lead to the discovery of other vital records such as baptisms, court attendances, settlement examinations or newspaper coverage. You can read more about this plotting process in the section on fairs and markets on p.26 and in the section on censuses on p.32.

The circuit was generally started in April and continued until October, meaning that you are likely to find your family on the road between those months. From October to April the family home might be in their tent or van on a permanent or semi-permanent encampment on the outskirts or in the centre of one of the major cities.

These fixed urban encampments - or 'Gypsyries' as they were sometimes referred to by the Gypsiologists - became increasingly numerous in the second half of the nineteenth century, being used as a stopping place not only during the winter but all year round, with different families using them as a base from which to travel. These Gypsyries owe their existence to the encroachment on Gypsies' traditional camping places in rural areas caused by the Enclosure Acts but also by the depopulation of rural communities and subsequent loss of customers for the Gypsies in the countryside and the growing attraction of large customer bases in industrial towns and cities.

Most large cities had at least one encampment. In London for example, there were large Gypsy communities in the Potteries at Notting Hill and in Battersea. In the

Birmingham area there was a large camp for over a quarter of a century on a piece of wasteland called 'Black Patch' on the border of Smethwick and Handsworth. In the area of Liverpool, there were favourite sites on the brickfields at Green Lane near Birkenhead and at Cabbage Hall and Walton Breck Road close to where Anfield Football Ground is today. In Blackpool, the Gypsy camp on the sand dunes at South Shore was an important tourist attraction from the 1840s until 1910 when the Gypsies were forcibly evicted by the growth of the Pleasure Beach Amusement Park which stands on the site to this day.[15]

Very young children and elderly members of the family might be left in such encampments all year round to save them the rigours of life on the road. Similarly a husband might travel alone or with other male relations and leave his wife and children in the camp. This may sometimes explain the absence of individuals from a family group in a census return.

As fixtures in the urban landscape and in the local community, the Gypsyries and their inhabitants were more likely to be captured in census returns. The registers of nearby churches and cemeteries may also record many Gypsy events. You may also find the interaction between the encampment residents and their non-Gypsy neighbours received press attention (as it frequently does in our own times) and that the names of Gypsies appear in newspaper reports. The archives of the modern-day Pleasure Beach in Blackpool, for example, include books of press cuttings dating from the first decade of the twentieth century which recount the long saga of the attempts of the authorities of Blackpool to remove the Gypsies from their South Shore encampment. Also included are cases of illegal fortune-telling and inter-family disputes which reached the local courts.

The annual volume indexes of the *Journal of the Gypsy Lore Society* (described on p.71) are a good source for the locations of many of these urban Gypsyries. George Borrow's *Romano Lavo-Lil*, published in 1874, includes descriptions of those in Wandsworth, the Potteries at Notting Hill and The Mount, Shoreditch, all in London.

In more rural locations, a modern-day reference to a 'Gypsy Lane' or a similar placename including the word 'Gypsy', 'Romany', 'Traveller', 'Tinker' or 'Pedlar' can be a good pointer to a location of a traditional stopping places for Travellers - their *'atchin tans'* - where they could be sure of being tolerated by local residents and landowners and so of remaining free from harassment. A convenient source of water and grazing for horses were key requirements. South London's 'Gipsy Hill' is a case in point. It marks the existence of a long-standing Gypsy encampment which the diarist Samuel Pepys visited and mentioned in his diaries which recorded his life between 1659 and 1669.

Such placenames - which are easily discovered through gazetteers and Ordnance Survey county atlases - can again provide a useful starting point for your searches in census returns or parish registers.

Fairs and markets

As so many Gypsy occupations involved buying and selling, a family's travels were generally plotted to take advantage of fairs and markets. The Easter Fair at Wanstead Flats, Essex, was known as the 'Gypsy Fair' because so many Gypsies from London and the eastern counties would make it their first gathering of the season.

In essence there were three specific types of fair or market but in many locations there was a natural overlap in the business carried on there. They were:

- Statute fairs: those held by ancient statutory right or charter in a particular locality for general trading business on a number of days a year.

- Hiring fairs: generally major annual events where farm servants would offer themselves up to farmers for a year's contract.

- Pleasure fairs which, as their name suggests, were largely for entertainment.

To these might also be added major race meetings, such as the Derby at Epsom (which started in 1779) and the National which was first run at Aintree in Liverpool in 1838 as the 'Grand Liverpool' steeplechase.

Locating trading fairs and markets

There are a number of sources you can consult to discover where and when fairs and markets took place.

Trade directories usually include the dates and/or days when fairs and markets took place and the kind of business carried out. This information is usually given in the general description of each town which heads the listings of residents and tradespeople.

Pat Loveridge has provided a valuable short-cut for researchers by using the information extracted from trade directories as her source to compile *A Calendar of Fairs and Markets held in the nineteenth century*. This contains a comprehensive survey of events from around England, Wales and Scotland, indexed by place, by date and by type.

There are also historic publications such as *Owen's Book of Fairs*. This gave a county-by-county breakdown of fairs and markets with full details of their date in the calendar, their duration and their type, as this extract of the horse fairs and 'pedlary' fairs for the county of Suffolk shows in 1817:

Aldborough
1 March, 3 May - toys

Beccles
Whit Monday, 2 October - horses and petty chapmen

Bury St Edmunds
Easter Tuesday and 2 October for three weeks

Debenham
24 June - braziers and toys

Lowestoft
12 May, 10 October - petty chapmen

Saxmundham
23 September - toys

Stradbrooke
21 September - toys

Sudbury
12 March, 10 July, 4 September - toys

Locating pleasure fairs

The history of pleasure fairs has also been extensively covered by many authors and such books often include national and regional calendars of events, one good example being Ian Starsmore's *English Fairs*.

Travelling showmen often disassociated themselves from Gypsies (and still do) - but there is clear evidence in their genealogies that many had Romani blood. If your ancestors had fairground connections, one of your prime sources for biographical information should be *World's Fair*: a weekly newspaper for travelling showpeople which has been published since 1904. You will find a complete run at the National Fairground Archive at the University of Sheffield and another at The Newspaper Library, Colindale, London. There are unfortunately as yet no name indexes to *World's Fair*.

In addition to Sheffield's important archive on the history of fairgrounds and showpeople, there is the Fairground Association of Great Britain to which enquiries about showpeople can be directed.

You may also find that your Gypsies were closely associated with one of the travelling menageries and circuses which travelled England and Wales in the nineteenth century and early twentieth century and sometimes appeared at pleasure fairs. Wombwell's and George Sanger's are among the more famous of these. If your travelling ancestors worked or performed in circuses, the Circus Friends Association or its associated mailing list may be able to provide information.

The evidence gathered from such sources as these may enable you to plot a possible annual circuit for your Gypsies. Knowing when and where they might be in a particular week or month could then lead to profitable searches in the appropriate parish registers for baptisms, marriages or burials, in census returns or in coverage in local newspapers.

Although there has been a considerable decline over time in the numbers of fairs and markets held throughout Britain, some of those which have traditionally been highlights of the Gypsy's year have been fiercely maintained and preserved by the Gypsies themselves, often in the face of severe opposition from *gaujos*. These fairs include the famous Appleby Fair which takes place at Appleby in Cumbria the week after Derby Day and the mid-May horse fair which takes place at Stow-on-the-Wold, Gloucestershire.

CHAPTER FOUR

Finding your Gypsy ancestors:
conventional family history sources

Gypsies of the past might have attempted to avoid 'capture' by the authorities in records whenever possible but they were obviously not always successful. This chapter therefore contains information on sources that most family historians conventionally use when searching for their ancestors. Although such sources are probably already familiar in their form and content, it is important when researching Gypsy ancestors to take a fresh approach to them in order to take account of the Gypsies' cultural and social differences.

Civil registration

The civil registration of births, marriages and deaths began in July 1837 in England and Wales. Microfiche copies of the original indexes are widely available in repositories such as the Society of Genealogists in London and in Record Offices and libraries both in Britain and in English-speaking countries abroad.

You will also find master indexes to births, marriages and deaths online. FreeBMD is in the process of compiling a free index stretching from July 1837 to 1983. Available at www.freebmd.org.uk, the index currently covers

the period up to about 1930 for all three events. For the years that FreeBMD has yet to tackle, the site offers access to digitised images of the original GRO index volumes so that you can conduct your own name searches quarter by quarter if you wish to.

For Gypsy family historians FreeBMD offers the particularly useful facility of being able to search by forename only. A blanket search of this kind for a Shipton, Ocean or Phoenix, for example, can be valuable for picking up related family members or for capturing individuals who may be using a surname alias on the day of registration.

The civil registration authorities in a number of English counties are working together with local family history societies to compile master indexes of the historic birth, marriage and death registrations for their own areas and making them available online. Lancashire (www.lancashirebmd.org.uk) and North Wales (www.northwalesbmd.org.uk) are just two of many examples. Searches can be conducted free and paid-for certificates ordered if required. The availability of indexes for other counties can be checked at www.ukbmd.org.uk

There are also a number of pay-per-view/subscription options. For example, the Ancestry site at www.ancestry.co.uk offers complete searchable indexes for the period 1837-2005. You can also view the pages from the original index volumes in digitised form.

Sight of these original index volumes is also available - again by subscription - at findmypast.com: www.findmypast.com

Births

A Gypsy child's birth may not be registered. In the early days of civil registration, in common with many non-Gypsies, Gypsy families may not have been aware that civil registration was necessary. Even when they did know, they seemed to neglect this responsibility throughout the nineteenth century and even well into the twentieth. You will also find instances where some children in a family were registered and others were not, for no apparent reason. Fortunately, baptism was an almost universal occurrence for Gypsy children so even if civil registration did not take place, all is not lost in attempting to trace a child's parentage - see the section on parish registers on p.43.

When a Gypsy child is registered, sometimes only the mother's name may appear on the certificate, even if she had a stable, long-standing partnership with the father.

The surname given to the child may be the mother's or the father's so you should search under both.

Marriages

Gypsies had their own marriage ceremonies and these held the same sanctity and importance for them as a formal church or register office ceremony. In some families - such as the East Anglian Shaws - virtually everyone married in church. But in others, even in the same region and in closely associated families, virtually no-one did. It is therefore important to consider both possibilities in your research and to reflect therefore that you may not always find marriage certificates for your own Gypsy ancestors.

There were some cases of couples who had spent their whole adult lives together marrying later in life after they had raised a number of children, possibly encouraged by well-meaning missionaries. This means that if you do undertake a search for a marriage, you may need to extend it well beyond the arrival of the first child.

When you do trace one Gypsy marriage in a particular church during the civil registration period, it can prove useful to consult the marriage registers themselves. In parishes where Gypsies found the parson sympathetic, you may find that a number of people in the same family or travelling group returned to use the church at different times.

Similarly, if families were enjoying an annual gathering of the clans at a particular location - for hop picking, for example - this would sometimes be taken as the ideal opportunity for a number of couples to marry in the same church on the same day.

Where and when Gypsy marriages did take place, they often attracted attention from local newspapers so a search through the press can be fruitful.

Deaths

Deaths were normally registered. Gypsy naming customs must however be kept in mind when searching through the civil registration indexes because a married woman or widow may be registered under her maiden surname.

Similarly, the forename registered at death may not always be that by which the person was known in life. As one typical example: a Gypsy baptised as Fabridge Smith and known by an abbreviation of this - Femi or Phebe - throughout her life was registered at her death as 'Elizabeth'. There is a taboo in Gypsy society about saying the name of someone who has died and it might therefore be conjectured that this is what the informant of the death had in mind in calling his late mother 'Elizabeth'.[16]

The misnaming may also be the fault of the Registrar. Family historians will no doubt be appalled to know that even in recent times there have been cases of Registrars of Births, Marriages and Deaths refusing to accept some Gypsy forenames because they consider them too outlandish. As one example: when a relative attempted to record the death of his aunt Vi Smith, the Registrar enquired what this was short for. When he was told 'Reservoir', he arrogantly refused this as a 'proper' name and declared that he would register her as 'Elizabeth': a move which will most likely prevent her descendants from ever tracing her death certificate, unless this story has been passed down to them.

As in the case of Gypsy marriages, the deaths and funeral ceremonies of Gypsies were often reported in local newspapers and even in national newspapers such as *The Times*.

Censuses

Most family historians reading this book will already be familiar with the contents and format of the returns which have resulted from the census of the population of England and Wales which has taken place every 10 years from 1841 to the present day with the exception of 1941. There are, however, a number of critical considerations for Gypsy family historians to take into account in their use of censuses which are rarely covered in general guides to this important source.

Census date
The census has been taken on a number of different dates in the course of its history. This can have an impact on whether or not you are likely to find your Gypsy ancestors in a particular year. The dates were:

- 1841 - 6 June
- 1851 - 30 March
- 1861 - 7 April
- 1871 - 2 April
- 1881 - 3 April
- 1891 - 5 April
- 1901 - 31 March
- 1911 - 2 April

As explained in the section on circuits and settlements, the Gypsies' travelling period of the year was generally from April to October. This means that in some census years many Gypsies would already be on the road rather than in a fixed place or in winter accommodation when the information was collected and so locating them may prove more difficult in some years than in others.

Location within the returns

1841
In 1841 the census enumerators were not required to take full census information from people who were not resident in houses. They were simply asked to count them by number and insert the information in a summary table at the front of the enumeration district book under 'Numbers of people in barns, sheds, tents and the open air.'

This means that you are likely to find tantalising entries such as 'nine people in tents, 5 men and 4 women' which was discovered in the census enumeration abstract for Amounderness Hundred (the present-day Blackpool area), indicating that there were Travellers in a locality but they remain totally nameless. You could however use this information as a pointer to local parish registers, Poor Law records or newspapers in the same area in the hope that the Travellers may have left their mark less anonymously in other documents at census-time.

You will however also find rare instances where enumerators have gone beyond their brief and have recorded Gypsies as fully as they have house-dwellers. If this is the case, you will generally find a mention of the existence of Travellers by number in the table at the beginning of the district and their personal details added at the very end of the enumeration district book.

1851
In 1851, census enumerators received the same directives as in 1841 on how to record those not in houses so you will again find tallies of numbers in Table B at the front of each enumeration district book. However some zealous enumerators fortunately took the trouble to record the full details of the Gypsies and other Travellers in their district. These will be recorded on the last page or pages of the enumeration district book.

1861
In 1861 there was a major improvement. Enumerators were ordered to collect full particulars from 'Persons not in houses' and list these under this heading at the end of the district.

1871-1911

From 1871 onwards, you should find Gypsies and other Travellers recorded in full in sequence among the house-dwellers in the actual street, lane or field where they were found.

If you find your Gypsy ancestors recorded in one census, it can be useful to refer to the same location in other censuses. It may be a place where they or their families regularly arrived, year in year out, on their circuit of a particular region or to attend a market or fair. (See the section on fairs and markets on p.26.)

Because Gypsies tended to travel as families or as inter-related groups, it is important when you find one family to scan through the same district looking for other Gypsies who may prove to be relatives.

Gypsies in houses

Naturally in all of the census years, if your travelling ancestors were living in a house or lodgings on census night, they should be recorded as house-dwellers in the normal sequence of the returns. It may only be their occupation or the wide geographical spread of the birthplaces of any children which indicate that they were usually itinerant.

Information given in censuses

- *Names*

  As explained earlier, Gypsies frequently used aliases, perhaps using both their mother's and their father's surname interchangeably depending on the situation or the location they were in. Many had nicknames or bye-names. If they were being forced to give a stranger their personal details, they were likely to suspect or misunderstand his motives and so be less than accurate in the names, ages and birthplaces they gave. The Gypsies' unconventional forenames were also likely to be misspelt by the enumerators. It is therefore vital not to ignore or dismiss Gypsies in census returns who seem familiar to you in the make-up of their family group yet who do not have the exact names you expect them to have. The 1851 example shown opposite is a case in point. The head of the household is in fact one Francis Smith. It is yet to be discovered why on this occasion he decided to adopt the name 'George Rix' - which is not a familiar Gypsy surname - when the other details he provides about his family are correct.

6. A census return for Old Buckenham, Norfolk, 1851, showing Table B and the corresponding entry for Gypsy families at the end of the enumeration district book (Crown copyright material in The National Archives reproduced by permission of the Controller of HMSO. Ref. HO 107 1822 folios 2 and 23)

- *Birthplaces*

Family historians are often advised not to rely too heavily on the information listed under 'Where Born' in census returns. This is even more true for Gypsy ancestors. Whereas settled ancestors are very likely to have been registered or baptised in the parishes they claim as their native place, nothing could be further from the truth for a Gypsy who may well have been born in one parish but baptised a week later in another parish after the family had travelled 40 or 50 miles further on. Some Gypsies may also claim their father's birthplace as their own or alternatively nominate a town which the family traditionally saw as its 'headquarters' - the place to which they might regularly return in winter months.

If the same birthplace is recorded for an individual in a number of census years, it is likely to be correct.

Census indexes

There are a growing number of finding aids for locating ancestors in census returns, particularly online.

- **Gypsies in census street indexes**

   The hard copy street indexes to large towns and cities (population 40,000+) which have been compiled by The National Archives and available in the search rooms at Kew, contain special entries for Gypsy encampments for the 1881 and 1891 censuses. These may be found under the headings of 'Caravans', 'Tents' and 'Gypsies'.

   Janet Keet-Black of the Romany and Traveller Family History Society has extracted and transcribed all the references to Gypsies and other Travellers found in these 1891 street indexes and these have been published by the Society in four volumes: see p.109 for contact details.

- **1911 census index**

Online

www.1911census.co.uk, www.findmypast.com and www.genesreunited.co.uk
Name searches are free but access to transcriptions of the census returns and to digitised images of them is on a by-subscription or pay-per-view basis.

This is the first British census release to give researchers sight of the forms that were completed by the heads of household themselves, rather than the enumerator's transcriptions of them. This means that you gain the advantage of seeing your own ancestor's handwriting and being able to gauge their level of literacy, as well as any errors they had made in their form-filling and crossed out. These very human mistakes - usually a result of mis-understanding the instructions - can provide invaluable extra information about the family and its members. Examples seen by the author for Gypsy families have included one where a father has added the birthdates of his children - day, month and year - in addition to their ages. In another, two sons have been listed along with their parents' names and then erased: both sons being married and living elsewhere with their wives and children. In a third, a daughter's name appears among her siblings but with 'Dead' poignantly added where her age should be.

Supplementary information about the make-up of the family unit has also been requested for the first time in this census. This promises a bonus for family historians. For a husband and wife, it includes the length of the current marriage, the number of children born alive to the marriage and - where appropriate - the number who have died: all important clues for subsequent searches for birth, marriage and death records.

- *1901 census indexes*

Online

There are five main commercial providers of indexes to the 1901 census for England and Wales, accessible on a by-subscription or pay-per-view basis. They are:

- Ancestry - www.ancestry.co.uk
- findmypast.com - www.findmypast.com
- TheGenealogist - www.TheGenealogist.co.uk
- GenesReunited - www.1901censusonline.com
- RootsUK - www.RootsUK.com

The book *Census: The Expert Guide* gives detailed reviews of what each provider offers in terms of search options, the index quality and image quality, plus useful charts that compare the different services. You can also check the extent of the index - that is, whether it's complete or partial - by visiting the sites themselves.

Commercial providers
There are five main providers of indexes to the 1881 census for England and Wales. Most offer free index searches and then access to transcriptions and/or original images on a by-subscription or pay-per-view basis:

• Ancestry - www.ancestry.co.uk
• findmypast.com - www.findmypast.com
• The Genealogist - www.TheGenealogist.co.uk
• GenesReunited - www.genesreunited.co.uk
• RootsUK - www.RootsUK.com

See the information under 1901 to help you decide which provider best meets your needs.

Index on CD-ROM

The Mormons' 1881 census index for England, Wales and Scotland is also available to purchase on CD-ROM and can be found in this form in many libraries and County Record Offices. By complementing it with the purchase of the Mormons' Family History Resource File Viewer Version 4.0, it is possible to search the data using keywords - such as 'Gypsy', 'tent' or 'tinker' - in addition to name or place searches. This makes it feasible to undertake a complete extraction of all Travellers from a particular region if required. This kind of blanket search will also alert you to instances where the enumerator has failed to collect the names of the Gypsies but has noted their existence and possibly listed them by gender and age.

• *1871 census indexes*

Online

Free index
There is some coverage of 1871 on FreeCEN at http://freecen.rootsweb.com. See the FreeCEN information under 1891 for details.

Commercial providers
There are currently six main commercial providers of indexes to the 1871 census for England and Wales, accessible on a by-subscription or pay-per-view basis. They are:

- Ancestry - www.ancestry.co.uk
- findmypast.com - www.findmypast.com
- TheGenealogist - www.TheGenealogist.co.uk
- GenesReunited - www.genesreunited.co.uk
- Origins - www.origins.com
- RootsUK - www.RootsUK.com

See the information under 1901 to help you decide which provider best meets your needs.

- ***1861 census indexes***

Online

Free indexes
There is some coverage of 1861 on FreeCEN at http://freecen.rootsweb.com. See the FreeCEN information under 1891 for details.

Free searches are also available at FamilySearch - http://pilot.familysearch.org. There are no digital images on this site, only transcriptions. But if you find something of interest, direct links take you to findmypast.com where you can see original documents by paying a fee. If however you are using a computer in a Family History Center, access to the images is free.

Commercial providers
There are currently six main commercial providers of indexes to the 1861 census for England and Wales, accessible on a by-subscription or pay-per-view basis. They are:

- Ancestry - www.ancestry.co.uk
- findmypast.com - www.findmypast.com
- TheGenealogist - www.TheGenealogist.co.uk
- GenesReunited - www.genesreunited.co.uk
- Origins - www.origins.net
- RootsUK - www.RootsUK.com

See the information under 1901 to help you decide which provider meets your needs.

- *1851 census indexes*

Online

Free index
There is some coverage of 1851 on FreeCEN at http://freecen.rootsweb.com. See the FreeCEN information under 1891 for details.

Commercial providers
There are currently five main commercial providers of indexes to the 1851 census for England and Wales, accessible on a by-subscription or pay-per-view basis. They are:

- Ancestry - www.ancestry.co.uk
- findmypast.com - www.findmypast.com
- TheGenealogist - www.TheGenealogist.co.uk
- GenesReunited - www.genesreunited.co.uk
- RootsUK - www.RootsUK.com

See the information under 1901 to help you decide which provider best meets your needs.

Index on microfiche

The Church of Jesus Christ of Latter-day Saints (Mormons) did a full name index and transcription of the 1851 census for three English counties as a test case when they were preparing to undertake their indexing of the 1881 census. The results of this - which cover Devon, Warwickshire and Norfolk - can be found on microfiche in genealogical libraries such as the Society of Genealogists.

- *1841 census indexes*

Online

Free index
At present you can access free transcriptions of the 1841 census for England and Wales at two sites:

- *FamilySearch - http://pilot.familysearch.org*
  As for 1861, this site holds transcriptions of all counties of England and Wales, but no digitised images. Again, direct links take you to the findmypast.com site

where you can view the original documents for a fee. If however you are using a computer in a Family History Center, access to the images is free.

- *FreeCEN - http://freecen.rootsweb.com*
  There is some coverage of 1841 on FreeCEN. See the FreeCEN information under 1891 for details.

Commercial providers
There are currently six main commercial providers of indexes to the 1841 census, accessible on a by-subscription or pay-per-view basis. They are:

- Ancestry - www.ancestry.co.uk
- findmypast.com - www.findmypast.com
- TheGenealogist - www.TheGenealogist.co.uk
- GenesReunited - www.genesreunited.co.uk
- Origins - www.origins.net
- RootsUK - www.RootsUK.com

See the information under 1901 to help you decide which provider meets your needs.

- ***Published census indexes***

Many family history societies have indexed the census returns for their own county or region and are offering them for sale in a number of formats: on microfiche, on CD-ROM and as printed books. Some societies hold their database themselves and offer search services on a fee basis.

Many such indexes are deposited at The National Archives, the Society of Genealogists, County Record Offices and local reference libraries.

To check the availability and whereabouts of census indexes, use Jeremy Gibson's *Marriage and Census Indexes*. The Society of Genealogists' *Census copies and indexes in the Library of the Society of Genealogists* can also be useful.

Parish registers

Registers of baptisms, marriages and burials have been formally kept by parishes since 1538 in England and Wales. Early volumes have often been lost or destroyed, but many parishes have records dating from the late sixteenth and early seventeenth centuries. There may be gaps in their coverage: for example, during the Civil War years and Commonwealth period.

Where the registers themselves are missing, you may find there are duplicates of their entries from 1598 in the form of Bishops' Transcripts. These were copies of the register entries compiled by the parish clerk and sent annually by each parish to the registrar of its diocese or archdeaconry.

Throughout their migration from India to the west, described in the Introduction, Gypsies have tended ostensibly to adopt the dominant religion of the country or countries through which they have passed or in which they have 'settled'. In England and Wales therefore the majority of the Gypsies of the past were Christians and have largely used the Churches of England and Wales for their baptisms, marriages and burials.

You may however occasionally find instances of Gypsy events in the registers of nonconformist denominations and Roman Catholic churches. Their choice does not necessarily mean that they were followers of the faith in question, rather that the chapel or church was the most convenient they could find or that the officials there offered them a warmer welcome than the local parish church minister.

In any register entries dating from before 1700, it is important to remember that Gypsies will often be recorded as 'Egyptians'.

Baptisms

Although Gypsies tended to avoid unnecessary dealings with non-Gypsies, the majority did approach the Church to have their children baptised. Some experts believe that 99% of all Gypsy children were recorded in this way, even if the process of civil registration was ignored. This is obviously a fortunate bonus for today's family historians.

One of the reasons why Gypsies opted for baptisms was undoubtedly to register a form of 'settlement' for a child. A family that was constantly on the move would find itself in severe difficulties under the Poor Law and Settlement Acts if it were not able to prove a formal attachment to a certain locality. An official written record of baptism in a register could be powerful evidence of a Gypsy's claim to a place of birth or settlement.

There could also be a financial benefit. It was often the custom for the clergy and other parishioners to provide a financial incentive or gifts in kind (such as clothing) to parents who were reluctant or saw no religious need to have their children baptised. This was no doubt the case when it was heard that a Gypsy child had been born in the parish or that there were Gypsy infants in a travelling group who had not yet been gathered into the Church.

This might explain why in some instances you may find a number of children in the same family or a number of children in the same travelling group being baptised together. It is therefore always important to take note of the names of other children baptised on the same day or in the few days on either side of a Gypsy child's baptism.

There is also clear evidence that some Gypsy families took advantage of the Church's missionary zeal. You often find the same child being baptised in two or more different parishes with a delay of a few days or a few weeks between the two. In one extraordinary case researched by Janet Keet-Black, one Gypsy couple indulged in 'serial baptisms' for their daughters and had them baptised on over 300 different occasions between 1831 and about 1840 in parishes as far apart as Devon and Yorkshire. The close proximity of parishes in and around London enabled them to have the same child baptised in a parish south of the Thames in Kent and north of the river in the City of London in the course of the same day. On some occasions, the father is recorded as being dead: a factor which undoubtedly attracted greater sympathy - and larger donations - from the parishes concerned.[17]

If a Gypsy family or travelling group received a particularly warm reception in a particular parish, they would often return to the same church in later years to have other children baptised there. So it is always useful if you find one baptism to scan through the register in other years before and after in search of siblings or other relatives. In a similar way, the same church might be selected as a venue for subsequent marriages.

If you are using a birthplace gathered from a census return to lead you to a place of baptism, be warned that this can often be a disappointing experience. A Gypsy may legitimately claim that he or she was born in a particular town or village but if the family broke camp and travelled on a few days after the birth, the new baby might have been baptised in a far distant parish and across a county border. A search of contiguous parishes is therefore always in order. Baptisms might also have been delayed until a family gathering - such as coming together for a fair or hop picking. In this case you may find several children of different ages being baptised together in the same church.

With reference to the entry itself, as in the case of civil registration, only the mother's name may be given, even if she had a permanent partnership with the father. This means that you will need to search both by the mother's surname and the father's. One bonus is that the information given in a baptismal register is very likely to be accurate as it was offered by choice and without compulsion by the Gypsy parents.

Regrettably you will also come across many Gypsy baptisms where the names of the child's parents are not given at all - and sometimes where the child itself is nameless, described only as 'a Gypsy child baptised'. It is difficult in these days of racial equality for us to comprehend the Church's dismissive attitude to a Gypsy child and its parents which seems evident in such an entry.

Even in cases such as these all may not be lost. If you have evidence that your family travelled in a particular region and had other children baptised in nearby parishes, a birthplace given in a census return may eventually enable you to give a name to the anonymous child by a process of elimination.

Marriages

As explained in the section on civil registration on p.29, some Gypsies never married formally in church or a register office, preferring instead their own ceremonies to mark and formalise a relationship.

As in the case of baptisms, when you find one Gypsy marriage in a particular parish, it can be useful to scan through the register in the years before and after the event to see if other Gypsy couples from the same family or travelling group were married there. Again, an annual gathering of a family at a location for a fair or harvest would make it an ideal occasion for a number of young couples to tie the knot.

When Gypsy marriages did take place, they often attracted much local interest. So it can be useful to turn to local newspapers for collaborative detail such as any additional ceremonies performed outside the church and descriptions of the costumes worn by the bride and groom.

Burials

There are many myths surrounding the burial of Gypsies. Some experts contend that the Gypsy's avoidance of authorities and a cultural fear of the dead and consequently of churchyards, led to many Gypsies being buried at the roadside or in secluded unmarked pieces of ground to which families were particularly attached.[18] There may have been isolated instances of this kind which would obviously go undocumented. But for the most part Gypsies were formally buried with all due ceremony and the rites of the Church in churchyards and public cemeteries.

As most family historians will already know, burials can be notoriously difficult to locate and the registers themselves disappointing in the amount of detail they give about the deceased. Often it is little more than name and age. This is generally the case for Gypsies as well as non-Gypsies, so identification can be difficult, particularly if your Gypsy has a conventional forename and common surname such as 'John Smith'.

You might be fortunate to find that the parish clerk has thought it fit to add that the deceased is a stranger. You may also discover, as in the case of baptisms, that the Gypsy is nameless, recorded simply, for example, as 'a Gypsy woman buried'.

A Gypsy's place of burial however had great significance for the family. It was often marked with a monument and became a place of pilgrimage on special occasions and anniversaries. You can read more about this in the section on monumental inscriptions on p.50.

As in the case of Gypsy marriages, Gypsy funerals attracted the attention of the press because they were often elaborate affairs and generally attended by large numbers of mourners - as this example from *The Times* of 14 August 1832 shows:

'*Death of the King of the Gipsies*
Died in a tent on our race-ground on Wednesday, the venerable Charles Lee, denominated 'King of the Gipsies'. The age of this Monarch of the murky tribe was not correctly known; they called him 74, but it is conjectured that he was much older. He has left about 50 children and grandchildren behind him. He was interred in St Ann's churchyard yesterday afternoon, followed by ten of his relatives, the rest of the family being absent at the different fairs, races etc, in the presence of 1000 spectators, who had from curiosity been attracted to the churchyard to witness the funeral of so exalted a character'. *Lewes paper.*

Finding aids

* *Parish register indexes*
  Many family history societies and individuals are in the process of indexing parish registers within their own county or locality. These indexes may be available to researchers on a fee basis, to purchase on microfiche, CD-ROM or in printed book form or accessible online.

National Burial Index
The Third Edition of the National Burial Index, published by the Federation of Family History Societies on CD-ROM in 2010, contains over 18 million burial records from 1538 to 2003 for counties throughout England and Wales. You can find out more at www.ffhs.org.uk/projects/nbi/nbi-v.3.php

Some of the counties which contributed to the Index have also made their databases of burials available at the by-subscription findmypast.com site: www.findmypast.com

FreeREG - http://freereg.rootsweb.com/cgi/Search.pl
This site offers free searches of millions of baptism, marriage, and burial records that have been extracted by volunteers from parish registers and nonconformist church records around the UK. You can search by surname on a county basis or a parish basis. The site advises that if you find an item of interest, you should always check the item in the original register as the online entry may not be a complete transcription. Visit the site to check on coverage for your county or region of interest.

findmypast.com - www.findmypast.com
This site offers searches of millions of baptisms, marriages and burials by subscription or on a pay-as-you-go basis. The Parish Records Collections includes entries from 1538 to 2005, including databases collated by family history societies that were originally held on the FFHS Family History Online site.

Ancestry - www.ancestry.co.uk
This by-subscription site contains some baptisms and marriages in the form of Pallot's Baptism and Marriage Indexes 1780-1837 and baptisms, marriages and burials for London parishes.

Origins - www.origins.net
This by-subscription site contains indexes to 7 million names from Boyd's Marriage Index, dating from 1538-1840. This is also an index to burials in London from 1538-1872.

Also try Jeremy Gibson's *Specialist Indexes for family historians* and *Marriage and Census Indexes for family historians* to track down locally held, hard copy indexes.

- **IGI and FamilySearch**

A generation ago it would have been virtually impossible for family historians to consider tackling their Gypsy family trees. At that time this would have meant travelling around the country to local archives and churches, picking parishes very much at random in the vain hope of chancing upon relevant baptisms and marriages.

This state of affairs was revolutionised by the arrival of the IGI: the International Genealogical Index, compiled by the Church of Jesus Christ of Latter-day Saints (Mormons) from their extracts of baptisms and marriages from Church of England, Church of Wales and nonconformist registers.

Originally published on microfiche on a county-by-county basis, the 1992 edition of the IGI is also available on CD-ROM at major repositories, enabling researchers to track their Gypsy ancestors easily across county borders. It is this facility which originally led to the discovery of the examples of multiple baptisms of Gypsy children referred to on p.45.

The same database is also available free online at www.familysearch.org where it has been augmented over the years by contributions by Church members. Here searches by forename only can be easily and quickly undertaken to ascertain their distribution or in cases where there is uncertainty as to whether a child was baptised under the father's or the mother's surname.

It is vital to use the IGI/FamilySearch only as a finding aid and also to remember that it may contain inaccuracies and omissions. It is understood that the majority of the nonconformist registers held under the references RG4 and RG8 at The National Archives have been entered in the IGI/FamilySearch. However, for parish registers it is by no means complete for any county of England and Wales, containing only entries extracted from those registers to which the Mormons have officially been given access and entries provided by private individuals.

Used with these caveats in mind, the IGI/FamilySearch in all its formats is invaluable. Cross-reference to the entry in the original baptismal or marriage registers will often provide useful additional information concerning occupations and places of abode, particularly in post-1813 registers. This can assist in confirming individuals as Gypsies and in plotting their travels. You may also find in the original registers that more than one child in the same family or in the same travelling group has been baptised on the same day.

The Church of Jesus Christ of Latter-day Saints has also published the results of more recent extracts from parish registers on CD-ROM for purchase by individuals. This British Isles Vital Records Index (2001 edition) contains over 10 million birth and baptism records and 1.9 million marriages from England, Wales, Scotland and Ireland dating from 1530 to 1906 and so provides a valuable supplement to searches in the IGI/FamilySearch. This database is now also available online here: http://pilot.familysearch.org

Marriage licences

Because of their travelling lifestyle, Gypsies who chose to marry in church were rarely able to satisfy the rules of residence which applied to marriage by banns and therefore sometimes applied for marriage licences.

The fact that a marriage by licence would cost considerably more than a marriage by banns and was often used by the upper classes as a means of demonstrating their wealth and avoiding unnecessary publicity, added a special appeal to the licence. It is therefore always useful to consult the indexes of marriage licences that have been compiled and published for many counties.

Documents relating to the issuing of marriage licences are generally held in Diocesan Record Offices. For details of the survival and whereabouts of licences and their indexes, consult Jeremy Gibson's *Bishops' Transcripts and Marriage Licences*.

Monumental inscriptions

The place where a Gypsy is laid to rest has always held more importance and significance for their families than it perhaps does for non-Gypsies. As well as being the only fixed point in a Gypsy's life, there are a number of taboos in Gypsy culture associated with death and the treatment of the dead, one of them being the need to provide a permanent abode for the spirit of the dead person - the *'mulo'* - so that it will not haunt the living.[19]

As a result of these beliefs, it was (and still is) common for a Gypsy's burial place to be marked with a monument, sometimes at considerable expense, and for the grave to be carefully tended throughout many generations. In addition, the funeral might be attended by hundreds of mourners.

This means that it is always useful to check any collections of monumental inscriptions recorded for the churchyards and public cemeteries in the areas in which your ancestors travelled. These may be held locally in County Record Offices, by family history societies or online.

There is also evidence to suggest that once a family had found a favourite burial spot they would then continue to have members of their family buried there for a number of years, even if this meant having to transport the bodies of the dead over considerable distances.

Gypsy families would sometimes make regular pilgrimages to burial plots on the anniversary of the death or at special times of year - such as Christmas - to pay their respects to the dead [20]. Knowing the date of death or burial you might therefore be able to pinpoint your family in a particular location at a particular time of year: again a useful pointer to the parish records in surrounding towns and, if the date is appropriate, census returns or newspapers.

As in the case of non-Gypsies, there was a great kudos in longevity. This means that the age at death recorded on a tombstone may have been elaborated on by relatives or, in the absence of documentary evidence such as a birth certificate, it may purely be an estimate.

Wills

Most non-Gypsies will be familiar with the funeral rite that involves the destruction of the possessions of a deceased Gypsy. You will find accounts even during the twentieth century of *vardos* being burnt and every item of clothing, jewellery and crockery being broken and secretly disposed of to prevent anything passing into the hands of relatives or souvenir-hunters. In earlier times, even the favourite horses and dogs of the deceased might be ritually slaughtered.

In some Gypsy families, an alternative or additional custom was to bury the dead in their best clothes and with some of their favourite possessions surrounding them in their coffins. This was done very much in the same style and with the same purpose as those of the ancient Egyptians: providing the dead with the means to continue their everyday life after death.[21]

These rituals can make Gypsy wills rare. It is usually only from the mid-nineteenth century onwards that there was a need for Gypsies to make a will as they invested in real estate or settled - but there may of course be exceptions. One case in point is the discovery by Gypsiologist David Smith not only of the will belonging to a Leicestershire 'tinker errant' Nicholas Leigh dating from 1632, but also of an inventory of his belongings [22] which poignantly includes '*Item: one blanket to cover him & his wife in ye night tyme as they chanced to lodge in Barnes or such places*' valued at eight pence.

Administration.

DEATH ON OR AFTER 1st JANUARY, 1898.

BE IT KNOWN that *William West*

of Back of Castle Inn Oswaldtwistle near Accrington
in the County of Lancaster

died on the *13th* day of *March* 1913,
at *Back of Castle Inn aforesaid*

intestate

That Sarah West his lawful widow and Relict has
renounced the administration of his Estate

AND BE IT FURTHER KNOWN that at the date hereunder written Letters of Administration of all the Estate which by law devolves to and vests in the personal representative of the said intestate were granted by His Majesty's High Court of Justice at the Principal Probate Registry thereof
to *Samuel Griper West of Back of Castle Inn*
aforesaid Licensed Hawker the Heir-at-Law

of the said intestate.
Reswon £5145

Dated the *26th* day of *September* 1913.

Gross value of Estate ... £*4462.8.0*
Net value of Personal Estate £ *nil*

(69,134). WL.33,088—112. 4000. 12/12. A.&E.W.
(74,100). „ 44,345—181. 3000. 3/13. „

7. A grant of letters of administration for the estate of William West who died in March 1913 in his *vardo* at the back of the Castle Inn, Oswaldtwistle, Lancashire, where he and his family had lived for a number of years (From the author's family papers).

Researchers should therefore not neglect the calendars of post-1858 wills and administrations held at the Principal Probate Registry in London and on microfilm or microfiche at many other repositories, nor the pre-1858 records of wills and administrations held in Diocesan Record Offices and at The National Archives. An index to the latter's collection of Prerogative Court of Canterbury (PCC) wills from 1384-1858 is available free online at www.nationalarchives.gov.uk/ documentsonline/wills.asp . Copies of original wills can be ordered for purchase from the same site.

Pre-1858 probate indexes for a number of English counties can be searched at Ancestry - www.ancestry.co.uk . This is a by-subscription service.

Newington-Irving's *Will Indexes and other Probate Material in the Library of the Society of Genealogists* may also be useful.

Newspapers

Many researchers who are new to Gypsy family history are surprised at the coverage their ancestors received in the local and even the national press, particularly in the nineteenth century.

The persecution and prosecution of Gypsies used to be reported then as extensively as it is today. Any court case involving Gypsies - no matter whether they were found innocent or guilty - tended to be reported more fully than those involving *gaujos*. These reports can provide invaluable additional details of names, ages, family relationships, occupations and travelling circuits which may not be available in the court records themselves.

This example from *The Times* of 25 November 1853 records a court appearance by self-styled 'Gipsy King' Elijah Boswell of Nottinghamshire. To add colour, the reporter also takes the opportunity to provide the reader with a potted genealogy of the Boswell family:

'A Royal Family - There is in the county of Nottingham an extensive tribe of gipsies headed by Elijah Boswell, who is styled the Gipsy King, a distinction which he is said to have literally inherited from a long line of ancestors. Four of the tribe - viz, Elijah and three of his sons - got 'into trouble' last week on account of a little matter of meum and tuum, and were brought before the Retford bench, which ended in Elijah and two of his sons being sent to the treadmill for one month, and the other son being committed for trial. The Gipsy King has been married three times and the following enumeration of his family is supplied from his own archives:

1. Eliza, born among the ling in Mansfield forest
2. Henrietta, born in Thieves'-dale-lane, near Osberton
3. Alfred, born in Treswell Back-lane
4. Walter, born on Kneesall-green
5. Adelaide, born in a lane between Langwith and Pleasley
6. Henry, born in a lane near West Stockwith
7. Lucy, born under Firbeck-park-side
8. Adam, born on Walesby-breck
9. William, born in Gamston-wood
10. James, born in Layard's Leap, between Newark and Sleaford
11. Elijah, born near Sturton High-house
12. Magnus, born in a lane near Langford
13. Riley, born near Bole guide-post
14. Alice, born in a lane, near Mattersey Gorse'

Subsequent research into this family has shown that the children's birthplaces are for the most part accurately recorded.

Equally, the exotic nature of Gypsy lifestyle and customs - for example, their weddings and funerals or the entertainment they provided at fairs and markets - also attracted the attention of the press and could receive extensive coverage.

Finding aids

Newspaper indexes

An index to *The Times* dating from its first issue in 1785 to the present day is available in book form at The Newspaper Library at Colindale, London, and at many major references libraries. Indexes for the years 1790-1905 and 1906-1980 have also been published on CD-ROM and are similarly widely available. This computerised version can be searched very quickly by personal name or topic. Keying in the word 'Gypsy' brings up dozens of references which can then be easily followed up in the microfilmed copies of *The Times* itself.

The Times' archives are also available online on a by-subscription basis at http://archive.timesonline.co.uk/tol/archive . Here you can search free by surname or keyword and view digitised images of original articles on payment of a fee.

Many local and regional newspapers have been indexed or are in the process of being so. These indexes may be found locally in County Record Offices or local studies centres in the form of card or computerised indexes. Some have been published. Others are increasingly being made available online.

One example of the latter is the British Library's collection of digitised national, regional and local newspapers for Britain and Ireland, covering the eighteenth and nineteenth centuries. Access to this collection is usually exclusively available from subscribing libraries and other institutions. However, in some counties of England and Wales - Oxfordshire, Lancashire and the City of London among them - if you are a member of a public library you can gain free access from your home computer simply by using your library card number. If your library provides this service, you may find you also get free access to *The Times* archives.

Specialist newspaper extracts collections

• *The Gypsy Collections, University of Liverpool*
These contain a comprehensive library of newspaper cuttings concerning Gypsies which were gleaned from the pages of the national, local, regional and international press. There are bound volumes covering the complete period 1895-1969 but more comprehensive in their coverage between 1907 and 1949. There are also loose cuttings dating from 1860 to the late twentieth century. Some of the cuttings are on microfilm. A name index is available as a computerised catalogue to researchers visiting the library. See the section on specialist archives on p.76 for more information.

• *'Affairs of Egypt' - Journal of the Gypsy Lore Society*
Summaries from the cuttings mentioned above were occasionally included in the *Journal of the Gypsy Lore Society* under 'Notes and Queries' and 'Affairs of Egypt': see the section on the *Journal* on p.69 for details of its whereabouts.

• *Blackpool Gypsies*
The archives of the Pleasure Beach in Blackpool, Lancashire, include a large number of press cuttings relating to the Gypsy encampment which stood on the current Pleasure Beach site at South Shore from 1840 to 1910.

• *Gypsies, Hawkers and other Travellers in the English South Midlands* and
• *More Gypsies, Hawkers and other Travellers in the English South Midlands & including East Anglia, The Home Counties and the South East*
As a by-product of his research into the personalities who provided music for social dancing in past centuries, Keith Chandler has collected numerous references from local newspapers to Gypsies, Hawkers and other Travellers who attended fairs and feasts in the eighteenth, nineteenth and early twentieth centuries.

These extracts have been published in book form in two volumes by the Romany and Traveller Family History Society. The first contains transcriptions of items from between 1744 and 1911 from newspaper titles in Berkshire, Bedfordshire, Buckinghamshire, Oxfordshire, Gloucestershire, Hertfordshire, Northamptonshire, Warwickshire and Worcestershire. The second volume covers the period 1759-1923 and broadens the geographical reach to also include newspapers in counties ranging from Cambridgeshire and West Kent to Hampshire.

Occupational records

Occupations governed by licences

Some of the occupations traditionally followed by Gypsies were subject to government regulation and required licences.

As one example, those for hawkers and pedlars* were first introduced in 1697. The National Archives hold registers of these Hawkers' Licences dating from 1697 to 1699. These contain information on 4,000 people but disappointingly few obvious Gypsy names.[23]

Licences and certificates were also issued by the Quarter Sessions for the following trades in the eighteenth and nineteenth centuries: pedlars, hawkers, chimney sweeps, higglers and kidders (hawkers of corn and meat) and badgers (dealers in corn and other foods).

For the whereabouts of Quarter Sessions records containing possible references to licences granted and details of those which have been printed, use Jeremy Gibson's *Quarter Sessions Records for family historians*.

From 1870 the responsibility for the licensing of pedlars and hawkers was passed to the Police. They were also responsible for issuing certificates to chimney sweeps, another trade that Gypsies sometimes followed.

It seems highly unlikely that many Gypsies of the eighteenth or early nineteenth centuries would have bothered to approach the authorities for a licence to trade. But as the nineteenth century progressed and such legislation became more vigorously enforced, you will find many Gypsies describing themselves in census returns, for example, as 'Licensed Hawkers' and should therefore find that their names are

---

* The difference between them is that pedlars travelled on foot and hawkers by horse.

COUNTY BOROUGH OF BOOTLE.

PEDLARS' ACT, 1871, 34 & 33 VIC. CAP. 96.

No. _3 4_

In pursuance of the above Act, this Certificate was granted to the undermentioned person, to act as a Pedlar, on foot, from _5th December_ 19_35_ to _4th December_ 19_36_.

Name _Percy Shaw_

Residence _The Caravan, Park Street, Bootle_

Trade or Calling _____

Age _79 years_

Height _5' 3"_

Hair _Black_

Complexion _Fresh_

Where Born _Blackburn_

Marks _nil_

[stamp: CHIEF CONSTABLE'S OFFICE 5 DEC 1935 BOOTLE]

Chief Constable.

[OVER.

8. The pedlar's certificate of Percy Shaw, granted to him in Bootle, Lancashire, in December 1935 (With kind permission of Percy Shaw's family).

included in licensing registers. Licensing of this kind has continued to the present day.

For information on what police records have survived and their whereabouts, consult Bridgeman and Emsley's *A Guide to the Archives of the Police Forces of England and Wales*, now available online. This gives a county-by-county listing of material that continued to be held by modern-day Police Forces in 1992, covering both licensing registers and criminal records, two random examples from it being:

* Huntingdon Constabulary
  Register of Pedlars 1877-1967

* West Riding of Yorkshire
  Pedlars' and Chimney Sweepers' certificates 1886-1930

In some counties, Police Forces have deposited their records with the local County Record Office. It is also worth checking if any indexing has taken place as in the case of the Devon Record Office where a joint project with the county's family history society has resulted in the publication of a *Register of Pedlars Certificates of the City of Exeter, 1871-1874* (Devon Family History Society, 2003).

Individuals who were discovered hawking without the necessary licence or without having their surname painted on their cart or wagon (as the law required), may be found on trial at court and subsequently appearing in reports in local or regional newspapers. See the section on newspapers on p.53 and the section on Gypsies and the law on p.64.

Trade directories

As Gypsies become increasingly more settled during the course of the nineteenth century, you may find them recorded in trade directories. Use the typical occupations listed in the section on occupations on p.19 as your guide to what headings to look under.

There are large collections of trade directories for the whole of England and Wales in the Society of Genealogists and in the Guildhall Library in London. County Record Offices and local studies centres usually hold directories for their own county or region. Electronic copies of directories on CD-ROM can also be purchased from a number of specialist publishers who advertise regularly in the British genealogical press.

Online you can find many directories for England and Wales in digitised form in the University of Leicester's Digital Library of Historical Directories at www.historicaldirectories.org. The by-subscription Ancestry site at www. ancestry.co.uk also has a large collection of directories available as digital images, searchable by name and keyword.

Military service

In his autobiography *The book of Boswell*, the ancestor that Silvester Gordon Boswell places at the head of his family tree is one Shadrack Boswell. He recalls that this great-great-grandfather was '*a soldier, evidently in the Press Gang of those days. He fought in Holland and was buried there*'. As Silvester Boswell continues his story, we hear that Shadrack's son Tyso Boswell was also pressed into military service early in the nineteenth century and that his son Wester's ability to read and write came from having his education funded by the government as a result.[24]

This case of Gypsies volunteering or being pressed into the armed services is not an isolated one - and in fact one Army officer writing in the *Genealogists' Magazine* in 1934 went as far as to claim that Gypsies were particularly attracted to military life and frequently served in the militia.[25]

There is evidence that they certainly did in times of war. During the Napoleonic Wars, the Gypsy Charles McLean was a member of the Bedfordshire Militia while his younger brother James was a Private in the Royal East Middlesex Militia and was killed at Waterloo.[26]

A century later, arm yourself with virtually any typical Gypsy surname and delve into the online indexes of First World War soldiers held on The National Archives site or at Ancestry.co.uk and you will find thousands of medal, service and pension records for Gypsies.[27] These include Silvester Gordon Boswell himself who, because of his unrivalled expertise in training and caring for horses, was drafted into the Veterinary Corps. In a similar way, many Gypsy men who were too old for active service were specially commissioned by the Army to keep them supplied them with horses.

The story of the life and sad First World War death of John Pateman's relative, the Kentish Gypsy soldier Walter Pateman, is recorded in his book *Seven Steps to Glory: Private Pateman Goes to War*. While *John's Story* by John Hearn, edited by his daughter Mary Horner, recounts his Second World War experiences in addition to life as a member of a Romany Traveller family with its roots in Chiswick and Ruislip, Middlesex.

For the whereabouts and contents of militia records, try Gibson's *Militia Lists and Musters 1757-1876*. For Army records, try William Spencer's *Army Records: A Guide for Family Historians* and *First World War Ancestors: A Guide for Family Historians*.

Freemasons and friendly society membership

For a people who largely kept themselves to the outskirts of society through their own choice, it is a curiosity that a number of Gypsy men were keen members both of the Freemasons and of similar 'friendly societies', such as the Royal Antediluvian Order of Buffaloes or 'Buffs'.

Some members of the Gypsy encampment at Blackpool's South Shore belonged to the local Buffs lodge at the end of the nineteenth century and their membership was of significant enough importance to them and their relatives to be recorded on their gravestones.[28] These are not isolated cases and registers of members of such organisations should therefore not be ignored, especially in locations where there were long-standing semi-permanent Gypsy encampments in the second half of the nineteenth century and the early twentieth century.

As another example: some members of the Boswell family reputedly belonged to Freemasons' lodges in England and Scotland. Registers of members of the Freemasons' United Grand Lodge of England can be searched for named individuals on payment of a fee.

See Roger Logan's *An Introduction to Friendly Society Records* and Pat Lewis's *My ancestor was a Freemason*. The online catalogue of the National Register of Archives at www.nra.nationalarchives.gov.uk/nra can also be useful for locating the whereabouts of surviving friendly society membership registers and other records.

Poor Law records

From the late sixteenth century until the first decade of the twentieth century, the relief of the poor in England and Wales lay principally in the hands of each parish or groups of parishes (called 'unions') and was governed by a number of Poor Law Acts. Throughout much of that period, it fell to the Overseers of the Poor in each parish to collect rates from the occupiers and owners of property and land and to use the funds to support and care for the poor, getting the unemployed back to work and removing and sending back to their own parish any passing strangers or vagrants who might try to claim support. As these 'passing strangers' naturally included Gypsies, valuable references to them are often found in records relating to the Poor Law. These include:

Vagrancy records

Many of the Poor Law Acts had provisions for the control and punishment of '*idle and disorderly persons, rogues and vagabonds and incorrigible rogues*'. Gypsies were covered by the 'rogues and vagabonds' definition so they often feature in documents recording arrests for vagrancy and any subsequent imprisonment, trial and punishment or removal. You can find them noted in:

- The accounts of Churchwardens, Overseers of the Poor and Parish Constables to be found among the papers belonging to individual parishes
- Removal orders ordering the conveyance of vagabonds to their own place of settlement (see below)
- Quarter Sessions records: accounts of the trial and punishment of vagrants
- The registers of Houses of Correction: where vagrants were held before their trial and possibly after, if they were found guilty of their charge.

Settlement examinations and removal orders

In 1662 the Settlement Act was passed. This was designed to control and regulate the movement of the entire population of Britain - but particularly the poor. As Travellers, Gypsies were at great risk of being caught contravening the Act and subjected to an examination by Justices of the Peace to discover their last legal place of settlement. This could be their place of: birth, apprenticeship, marriage to a settled parishioner, employment for over a year, residence in a property with an annual rental value of more than £10 or service as a parish officer (such as Overseer of the Poor or Churchwarden).

There are obviously very few of these conditions that Gypsies could fulfil, apart from place of birth - which perhaps helps to explain why they were traditionally so keen on having their children formally baptised.

The documents recording the process of settlement examinations, orders and removals can contain biographical information, sometimes recorded verbatim. This might include:

- The name of the Traveller and that of his/her partner and children
- Their ages
- Marital status
- Occupation
- Place(s) of birth
- The place where they claimed to be legally settled

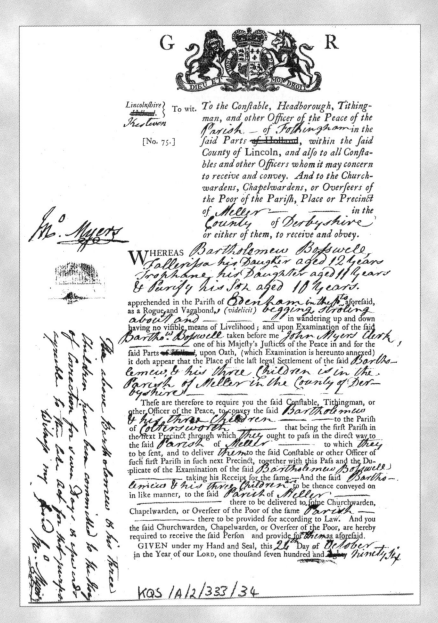

G R

Lincolnshire } To wit. To the Constable, Headborough, Tithing-
~~Holland~~   man, and other Officer of the Peace of the
Kesteven   Parish of Fothingham in the
                        said Parts ~~of Holland~~, within the said
[No. 75.]   County of Lincoln, and also to all Consta-
                        bles and other Officers whom it may concern
                        to receive and convey. And to the Church-
                        wardens, Chapelwardens, or Overseers of
                        the Poor of the Parish, Place or Precinct
                        of Meller   in the
                        County   of Derbyshire
                        or either of them, to receive and obvey.

Jn.o Myers

WHEREAS Bartholomew Bosswell
Tollerissa his Daughter aged 12 Years
Trophane his Daughter aged 11 Years
& Purify his Son aged 10 Years.
apprehended in the Parish of Edenham in the p.ts aforesaid,
as a Rogue and Vagabond, (videlicit) begging, strolling
about and   in wandering up and down
having no visible means of Livelihood ; and upon Examination of the said
Barth.w Bosswell taken before me John Myers Clerk ,
one of his Majesty's Justices of the Peace in and for the
said Parts ~~of Holland~~, upon Oath, (which Examination is hereunto annexed)
it doth appear that the Place of the last legal Settlement of the said Bartho-
lemew, & his three Children is in the
Parish of Meller in the County of Derbyshire

These are therefore to require you the said Constable, Tithingman, or
other Officer of the Peace, to convey the said Bartholomew
& his three Children   to the Parish
of Colterssworth   that being the first Parish in
the next Precinct through which they ought to pass in the direct way to
the said Parish of Meller   to which they
to be sent, and to deliver them to the said Constable or other Officer of
such first Parish in such next Precinct, together with this Pass and the Duplicate of the Examination of the said Bartholomew Bosswell
taking his Receipt for the same. And the said Bartho-
lemew & his three Children to be thence conveyed on
in like manner, to the said Parish of Meller
there to be delivered to some Churchwarden,
Chapelwarden, or Overseer of the Poor of the same Parish
there to be provided for according to Law. And you
the said Churchwarden, Chapelwarden, or Overseer of the Poor, are hereby
required to receive the said Person and provide for them as aforesaid.
GIVEN under my Hand and Seal, this 21 Day of October
in the Year of our Lord, one thousand seven hundred and ~~ninety four~~ ninety six

KQS / A / 2 / 333 / 34

9. The settlement examination of Bartholomew Bosswell and three of his children from Kesteven Quarter Sessions, Lincolnshire, Epiphany 1797, which led to him being returned to his parish of settlement in Derbyshire. His partner Mary Buckler and three other children were examined at the same time and dispatched to Wiltshire (With the kind permission of Lincolnshire Archives. Ref. KQS A/2/333/34).

This extract from an eighteenth century example clearly shows how valuable a find of this kind can be. It involves a Gypsy named Damon Draper (sometimes known as 'Lee'), arrested for vagrancy in North Hampshire in 1796 and gives not only a pen-portrait of Damon but a rare insight into his lifestyle: his choice of accommodation, his travelling companions and the routes he regularly followed in search of work.

The Examination of Damon Draper taken this Thirteenth Day of February 1796
Who being brought before me as a Rogue and Vagabond...Declareth That his Name is Damon Draper and That He is a Razor Grinder and Tinker and sometimes has Rented a Lodging at Deptford in Kent at Eighteen Pence a Week; That He left the Same with his Wife Frances late Frances Lee who is now Present, sometime before Christmas last, and since That They both have accompanied Elizabeth Lee, wife of Edward Lee, their Sister and Have from that Time led the Life of a Vagrant, Lying abroad under Hedges and in Woods and Lanes and in no Settled or fix'd Residence.

The said Damon Draper further Declareth That He was Born as He has heard and Believeth at Corsham in the said County of Southampton, but that he does not Know whether His Mother was Married or not. But this Examinant Declareth that He was married to his present Wife Frances on a Monday, about Eight Years ago at Branchley near Cranbrook in Kent; and That it was in the Hop-Picking Season...The said Elizabeth [sic] Draper saith That She was born at Walton upon Thames in Surry, and that her Father's Name was John Lee, and her Mother's Name was Jemima.
(Source: Hampshire Record Office, Reference No. 44M49/G3/797/2)

Settlement documents are usually found in County Record Offices, catalogued by parish. In some counties you may find they have been indexed by the Record Office or local family history society and are available as card indexes, online indexes or in published book form. The settlement indexes of Lincolnshire and Hertfordshire are two examples of the latter.

Poor house and workhouse records

In Gypsy culture elderly relatives were, for the most part, cared for and supported in their old age by their extended family. You will however occasionally find individuals in poor house and workhouse records. This might have happened when the family fell on particularly hard times or when the older person needed medical care or accommodation while younger members of the family were on the road.

Typical surviving records from poor houses and workhouses include admission books (which give name, sex, age and date of admission and departure) and birth, death and burial records. Workhouses were also enumerated in censuses so you might be lucky enough to find Gypsy relatives listed among the inmates.

To discover the whereabouts of existing Poor Law records and their indexes, use Jeremy Gibson's *Poor Law Union Records* and *Specialist Indexes for the family historian*.

Gypsies and the law

Records relating to the legal processes of England and Wales are a particularly useful source for Gypsy family historians. This is not because Gypsies were less law-abiding than *gaujos* but rather because, as explained earlier, Gypsies were subject for centuries to a large body of legislation* which was pointedly anti-Gypsy in that it was designed to put a stop to movement, hawking or camping on the highway. Until as late as 1783, it was a capital crime even to be a Gypsy.

The result is that Gypsy family historians run a better than average chance of finding references to ancestors in Quarter Sessions records, Assizes records and the registers of local Houses of Correction and County Gaols, and also in newspapers which reported on court hearings and sentencing.

Overview of legal records

For an excellent general guide to the criminal records of England and Wales and their whereabouts, consult David Hawkings' *Criminal Ancestors*.

Police records
The records held by Police Forces relating both to the licensing of hawkers and chimney sweeps and to criminals may be held by the Police Forces themselves or deposited with County Record Offices. They are generally subject to a closure period of between 30 and 70 years. Use Bridgeman and Emsley's *A Guide to the Archives of the Police Forces of England and Wales* - available online - to ascertain their content.

The county of Sussex has a unique set of records relating to Gypsies called 'The Gypsy Diaries'. Dating from 1898 to 1926, these journals were compiled by six police divisions to record the comings and goings of Gypsies and other Travellers passing through the county and any complaints made against them. The information which includes hundreds of family names has been indexed by Janet Keet-Black and published by the Romany and Traveller Family History Society.[29]

* A summary of this legislation is given in Appendix 1 on p.91.

Assize Court Records
The records for England and Wales are held at The National Archives. Hawkings' *Criminal Ancestors* provides a comprehensive survey of their organisation and content.

In the county of Middlesex and the City of London the place of the Assize Court was taken by The Old Bailey. The Session Papers of The Old Bailey 1674-1913 have been indexed and are available online at www.oldbaileyonline.org complete with digitised images of the original court documents themselves. This is a free-to-view site.

Quarter Sessions Records
These are generally held by County Record Offices. Some have been indexed and/or published. Jeremy Gibson's *Quarter Sessions Records* will guide you to their whereabouts. A name search online using the Access to Archives (A2A) site at www.nationalarchives.gov.uk/a2a can also be useful. This database includes brief summaries of Quarter Sessions cases for many counties.

Petty Sessions Records
Petty Sessions have been held in some counties since the sixteenth century. In the eighteenth, nineteenth and twentieth centuries they were routinely used - as the name implies - for trials relating to minor offences, from the use of obscene language and drunkenness to allowing horses to stray. Where these records survive, they are generally in County Record Offices.

Criminal Register: online index to those tried at Quarter Sessions and Assize Courts, 1791-1892
The names of those who were charged with a crime for trial at the Quarter Session or Assize Courts of England and Wales in the period 1791-1892 are recorded in the Criminal Register. The original Register is held at The National Archives at Kew, London, but in 2009 it was digitised and name-indexed by Ancestry and is now available to researchers online on a by-subscription basis. The Register lists each individual's crime, place and date of trial and the sentence, if convicted. Those acquitted appear here too. It therefore provides a useful shortcut way to identify which court records - and which local newspapers - you need to search and when.

Transportation

Around 212,000 people were convicted to be transported to Australia between 1788 and 1868. Of these only a tiny percentage had Gypsy blood but it can nevertheless be worthwhile to check if any members of your family were sent 'Down Under'. This is because the biographical information recorded about convicts can be comprehensive: from height, hair colour and tattooes to the whereabouts of the family they have left behind.

Some Record Offices and local family history societies have extracted and published indexes to those individuals tried and sentenced to transportation within their counties. As two examples: the Lincolnshire Record Office has produced both a printed guide and an online index, while the Hertfordshire Family History Society has published a book.

David Hawkings' *Bound for Australia* gives details of the records relating to transportees to Australia between 1788 and 1868 which are held both in Britain and in Australia.

Online there are a number of indexes of convicts transported to New South Wales, Van Diemen's Land (Tasmania) and Western Australia. A good starting point for checking what's available is www.CyndisList.com/prisons.htm

By-subscription sites such as Ancestry (www.ancestry.co.uk) offer not only name indexes but also access to digitised images of some of original convict documents, one example being the Australian Convict Transportation Registers 1791-1868. The Ancestry site also includes Convict Musters for New South Wales and Tasmania 1806-1849 (the equivalent of census returns) and a partial index of those transported to New South Wales and Western Australia. The latter offers the advantage of being searchable by occupation only: a process that can throw up individuals of possible Gypsy blood who are not immediately apparent by their surname alone.

For Gypsy transportees of earlier times, try checking Peter Wilson Coldham's *The Complete Emigrants in Bondage 1614-1775*. Published both in book form and on CD-ROM, this provides a comprehensive (though not complete) listing of those sent to the Americas after sentences of transportation were passed on them in English and Welsh courts. There were possibly as many as 50,000 people in total, non-Gypsy and Gypsy.

The author has a special interest in transported English Gypsies and holds an index of them - see the indexes section on p.82 for details.

Emigration

The draw of America as 'the land of opportunity' proved as strong for British Gypsies as it did for their non-Gypsy counterparts in times past. Consult the family trees compiled by the Gypsiologists in the nineteenth and early twentieth centuries and you are likely to see many individuals recorded as having emigrated and being 'in the USA' or 'in Canada'. This means that even if you are convinced that your own direct ancestors never left Britain, you should not neglect family history sources on the other side of the Atlantic, particularly if these are easily accessible online.

This is because you may find that if siblings of your ancestors emigrated, the American or Canadian documents recording their life events - such as marriage or death - may contain biographical information that is not usually included in the counterpart English or Welsh records. As one example, a Canadian marriage record can include the names of both the father and the mother of the bride and groom. While passenger lists recording the arrival of immigrants in American ports or documenting individuals crossing the US/Canadian border sometimes give the name and address of the next of kin left in the country of origin.

The newspapers of North America, like British ones, showed a deep fascination in Gypsy life - and not only the life of Gypsies who were resident in the USA and Canada. Search an online index to an historic newspaper in either country - such as New York's *Brooklyn Daily Eagle* at http://eagle.brooklynpubliclibrary.org - using 'Gipsies', 'Gypsies' or 'English Gipsies' as your search terms. You are likely to find dozens of articles, some describing families who had emigrated from Britain to the USA but also some looking at different aspects of the everyday lives of English and Welsh Gypsies in their native countries.

There may even be photographs. Examples of articles in the *Brooklyn Daily Eagle*. include ones showing the encampments of British families who were travelling in and around New York at the turn of the twentieth century, including named individuals. While a long account about Gypsy hop-picking traditions in Kent shows their living accommodation. Both index searches and sight of the original articles for this particular newspaper are free.

Online indexes

Ellis Island - www.ellisisland.org
A free index of those who entered the USA via the Ellis Island immigration station in New York between 1892 and 1924.

Ancestry - www.ancestry.co.uk
This by-subscription site offers name indexes to a range of records for passengers entering the USA and Canada via different ports or crossing the US/Canadian border.

findmypast.com - www.findmypast.com
This by-subscription/pay-per-view site offers indexes to passenger lists for those leaving the UK in the period 1890-1960, with destinations ranging from North America and Australia to South Africa.

British Gypsies in US census records
http://lockeroots.home.comcast.net/~lockeroots/GypsyCensusRecords.html
Search here free for extracts from US censuses that include members of Gypsy families originating in Britain.

CHAPTER FIVE

Finding your Gypsy ancestors: special
sources for the Gypsy family historian

As explained in the Foreword, family historians with Gypsy ancestors owe a great debt to the Victorians. Their passion for exploration sparked off a number of important new sciences such as anthropology and ethnography. While some enthusiasts travelled the world to discover and record the culture, customs and lifestyle of native peoples, others discovered a fit subject for study much closer to home in the Romani Gypsies of Britain.

This section introduces the surprisingly large body of information that now exists as a direct result of those studies - and which can by paradox help family historians to discover far more about their secretive and elusive Gypsy ancestors than they possibly can about their non-Gypsy ancestors.

Journal of the Gypsy Lore Society

The most important of all the special sources for the Gypsy family historian is the *Journal of the Gypsy Lore Society* - known as the *JGLS*.

The Gypsy Lore Society was founded in Britain in May 1888 by a group of academics who wanted a means of recording, preserving and broadcasting the history and the culture of the Gypsy, both the Gypsies of Britain and those elsewhere in the world.

Their *Journal* first appeared in July 1888 and has been published largely on a quarterly basis in five series (with a number of gaps) to the present day. The series of greatest value to family historians with English or Welsh Gypsy ancestors, because of the substantial amount of genealogical and anecdotal material they contain, are:

- Old Series, July 1888-April 1892
- New Series, July 1907-1916
- Third Series, 1922-1973

As an example of the type of material to be found in the *JGLS* of value to family historians, this is an extract from the contents list of a single issue, dated January 1910 (New Series Volume III No. 3), together with one of the important Gypsy family trees it contains - shown on p.72:

Borrow's Gypsies
Gypsy Forms and Ceremonies
A Bulgarian Gypsy Folk-Tale
A Contribution to French Gypsy History
A Pilgrim's Progress: commemorating the life of 'deep Romany' speaker Edwin Buckland who died in 1863 aged 75
Notes & Queries:

- Addenda to Borrow's Gypsies
- Funeral Libations
- Visions and Dreams
- Signs and Omens
- British Gypsy Crimes

Much of the information relating to the family histories, customs and culture of Gypsies in the British Isles was gathered as oral history from Gypsies themselves. As is often the case with oral history, few of the references or family trees contain precise dates of events. Some have been found on further research to have occasionally 'telescoped' the chronology of events: for example, by treating a father and son of the same name as one individual.

As the information was generally gathered from people who were unable to read or write, the names of individuals are recorded as they were heard and understood by the collector and so may not be totally accurate. Similarly, the memory of those Gypsy descendants who were called upon to remember the names of ancestors or distant relatives of 150 years earlier may occasionally be hazy or at fault.

Despite these minor reservations, Gypsy family historians can count themselves extremely fortunate to have been bequeathed such a treasure of genealogical information. For the most part you will find that the substance of the genealogies and related family stories recorded in the *Journal* generally stand the test when cross-checked against the hard documentary evidence of parish registers and census returns.

The information can therefore be used as a valuable starting point and guide to one's own research in original sources - always working with the caveat that the 'facts' represented on the printed page may have been subject to misinterpretation or speculation on the part of the non-Gypsy recording them.

In the opinion of the author it is not overselling the importance of the *Journal* to suggest that no Gypsy family historian should contemplate starting their research without first consulting this publication.

Finding aids for the *JGLS*

- *Volume indexes*
  An annual index was published for each volume in the Old, New and Third Series mentioned above. These indexes are far more comprehensive in the years before the Second World War where they give page references to all the individuals named in the text as well as general subjects. The indexes in later volumes tend not to include personal names.

- *Series indexes*
  There is a single index to all the volumes in the Old Series (1888-92), published in 1914. In the same year George Black published *A Gypsy Bibliography* which is a comprehensive guide to the majority of the books and articles on Gypsy subjects published worldwide before 1914. This therefore includes the contents of the *Journal* up to that time.

- *Name index in progress*
  The Romany and Traveller Family History Society is working on an accumulative name and occupation index for the complete run of the Old, New and Third Series. This will be announced on the Society's Website and quarterly journal when it appears.

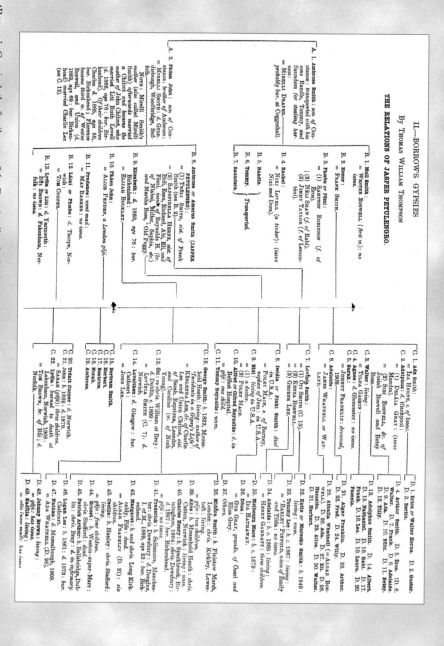

10. 'Borrow's Gypsies': the family tree of the East Anglian Smith family published in the *Journal of the Gypsy Lore Society*. The *Journal* contains many such trees gathered as oral history in the nineteenth and early twentieth centuries (Ref. *JGLS* New Series Volume III No. 3, January 1910).

Where to find the *JGLS*

Part or complete holdings of the *Journal* for the years 1888-1973 are to be found in a number of major repositories in Britain. In 1994 the *British Union Catalogue of Periodicals* (1994) listed their availability at the locations listed below.

You can also check the specific volumes that each library holds by visiting the Copac Website (National, Academic and Specialist Library Catalogue) at http://copac.ac.uk and using *'Journal of the Gypsy Lore Society'* as your search term on the home page. Searches of this Catalogue are free.

However, in all cases researchers are advised to contact libraries before visiting in order to check holdings before making a special visit. There have been a number of alarming instances in recent years of libraries selling off their *JGLS* collection because it has been under-used!

Public reference libraries
Birmingham Public Library
Edinburgh Public Library
Central Library - Kensington, London
Central Public Library - Liverpool
Manchester Public Library

University libraries
Birmingham University Library
Cambridge University Library
Glasgow University Library
University of Leeds*
University of Liverpool*
University of London:
  • Folk Lore Society, University College
  • School of Oriental Studies
University of Nottingham Library
University of Oxford - Bodleian Library*

National libraries
British Library - London
National Library of Scotland - Edinburgh
National Library of Wales - Aberystwyth

* There are special Gypsy collections at these libraries, described on pages 76-80.

Specialist archives

The Gypsy Collections, University of Liverpool

The Gypsy Collections at the University of Liverpool are one of Britain's three principal archive collections on Gypsies. They comprise the Archive of the Gypsy Lore Society 1888-1973 (see p.69 for information about the Gypsy Lore Society) and the Scott Macfie Gypsy Collection. Between them these amount to over 50,000 items relating principally to the history, the customs and culture of the Gypsies of the British Isles but also including the Gypsies of Continental Europe.

Of particular importance to Gypsy family historians are the Collections' manuscript genealogies which relate to many of the major British Gypsy families. These were generally collected as oral history during the late nineteenth and early twentieth centuries and are available to researchers in the form of folders of original notes and notebooks and as genealogical notes contained in correspondence. Of particular importance for the accuracy of their genealogical facts are the letters of T W Thompson. The notes of the Reverend George Hall - the 'Hall Papers' - have been filed into folders by surname and catalogued as follows:[30]

Ayres	Gray	Ryles
Baker	Hall	Scamp
Booth	Heron	Seeley
Boss	Ingram	Shaw
Boswell	Joules	Sheriff
Boyling	Lee	Small
Brown	Lock	Smith
Buckley	Lovell	Taylor
Burton	Mace	West
Clayton	Morrison	Wharton
Deadman	Palmer	Williams
Draper	Parker	Wilson
Evans	Pinfold	Winter
Gaskin	Robinson	Wood

As an introduction to the Gypsy Collections, the University of Liverpool Library is publishing a series of 'Gypsy name packs' based on the above list, each containing a representative sample of what the Collections hold on a specific surname: eg, manuscript family trees, press cuttings, catalogue lists of photographs and so on. Contact the Gypsy Collections for the current availability list: see p.107 for contact details.

Other key sources for family history information in the Collections include:

- *The Journal of the Gypsy Lore Society* (1888 to the present) - see p.69
- Photographs and transparencies of named Gypsies, dating mainly from about 1900 to the 1940s but with some earlier examples
- Correspondence of the Gypsy Lore Society 1908-73 and its leading members, containing much useful genealogical information about Gypsy families
- Newspaper and magazine cuttings relating to Gypsies, 1860s to the late twentieth century (see p.55 for more information)
- Over 12,000 printed works about Gypsies, both non-fiction and fiction
- Vocabularies of Romani languages, including Anglo-Romani and its regional dialects and the Romani of Wales.

The Hall Papers, the correspondence and the newspaper cuttings have all been indexed by surname and these indexes are available for searches by personal visitors to the Collections as computer databases.

The Gypsy Collections are open to family historians by appointment. Their contact details are given in the useful addresses section on p.107 or see their Website at http://sca.lib.liv.ac.uk/collections/colldescs/gypsy/index.htm.

The Romany Collection, Brotherton Library, University of Leeds
The second of Britain's principal Gypsy collections, the Romany Collection forms part of the Brotherton Library at the University of Leeds. Collected and donated to the Brotherton by Dorothy Una Ratcliffe (the niece-in-law of the Library's founder, Lord Brotherton, and an enthusiastic Gypsiologist and author herself), it contains important works relating to the historical, social and linguistic aspects of Gypsy life in Britain and worldwide with particular focus on those appearing in the nineteenth and early twentieth centuries. The printed material is complemented by a varied collection of music, letters, manuscripts, play-bills, pictures, engravings and other objects relating to Gypsy culture.

A catalogue of the Collection was published in 1962 and is a useful starting point for determining the scope and the contents of the Collection, although much has naturally been added to it since that date.

The Romany Collection is open to family historians by appointment. Their contact details are given in the useful addresses section on p.107 or see their page at www.leeds.ac.uk/library/spcoll/virtualtour/side_romany.htm.

The Robert Dawson Romany Collection, Museum of English Rural Life Library,
University of Reading

The third of Britain's great Gypsy collections was created over many years by Robert Dawson - one of the foremost modern-day Gypsiologists - and donated to the Romany and Traveller Family History Society in 1998. In February 2000 the Society deposited the Collection on permanent loan to the Museum of English Rural Life Library of the University of Reading in order to make it more easily accessible to Society members and other bona fide researchers.

Known as The Robert Dawson Romany Collection, it includes:

- Printed books
- Unpublished manuscripts
- Music on cassette, CD and record
- Correspondence
- Paintings, illustrations and postcards
- Magazine articles
- Notebooks on Gypsy families
- Videos
- Ephemera
- Photographs
- Examples of English Gypsy crafts

An almost complete run of the *Journal of the Gypsy Lore Society* (1888 to the present) was deposited as part of the Collection in late 2010.

The Museum of English Rural Life is a unique resource for the study of the history of English rural life and is open to the public. There is an online catalogue to its holdings but as cataloguing of The Robert Dawson Romany Collection itself is in progress, researchers are advised to contact the Museum (see the useful addresses section on p.107) to check on the availability of individual items and to make an appointment.

You can read more about the Collection and see a catalogue of the non-fiction printed books it contains by visiting the website of the Romany and Traveller Family History Society at www.rtfhs.org.uk

Although not specialising in Gypsy archives, the Bodleian Library of Oxford University holds a number of important Gypsy items in its Modern Manuscripts Collection. This is partly due to the fact that one of the foremost Gypsiologists of the twentieth century, Eric Otto Winstedt, was at one time the Librarian there. Examples include:

- The Thompson Papers: a major collection of manuscript notebooks, papers and Gypsy pedigrees and genealogical information collected by the leading Gypsiologist T W Thompson and bequeathed by him to the Bodleian on his death in 1968

- A collection of photographs which reportedly was once a duplicate of that held at the University of Liverpool but is now believed to be more complete than Liverpool's.

Among the printed works of Gypsy interest in the Library are copies of the *Journal of the Gypsy Lore Society* (1888 to the present).

The Bodleian's Catalogue of Printed Books can be consulted on CD-ROM in major reference libraries such as the Guildhall Library in London and also online.

The Bodleian Library is open to family historians by appointment. Contact details are given in the useful addresses section on p.107.

Education and edification

The story of the persecution and prosecution of Gypsies in Britain has been briefly covered in the historical introduction.

At the end of the eighteenth century the authorities switched their tactics from attempting to eradicate the Gypsies to their reformation. The aim was to convert Travellers from what was viewed as their godless, wayward lifestyle to life as members of settled society.

Education and religious instruction were key elements of this conversion process as the Church and other benevolent organisations saw it. We therefore see the start of a missionary crusade to improve the lot of Gypsies. This ran throughout the nineteenth century and well into the twentieth century in various bursts of intensity:

David Mayall's *Gypsy-travellers in nineteenth century society* provides a comprehensive account of this evangelical movement.[31]

Records of the work of these Gypsy missions do not generally contain information of direct use in establishing a genealogy, as the names of Gypsies attending meetings are usually not given. However, some exceptions may be found such as the 1882-3 diaries of the Reverend T E Holt which have been published by the Wiltshire Family History Society as *Travelling Folk: Itinerant Mission in the Diocese of Salisbury, 1882-1883* and also in its companion volume *Parish on Wheels* by J H Swinstead, a reprint of a book originally published in 1897.

When it comes to education, in some locations you may find that schools were established exclusively for Gypsy children to aid the reformation process. One such school was founded in 1847 in Farnham, Dorset, and was captured on the census of 1851 containing a dozen named pupils and a governess.[32] Another in Shalford, Surrey, established at the end of the nineteenth century by Louisa, Lady Sitwell, is mentioned in 'Notes & Queries' in the *Journal of the Gypsy Lore Society*.[33]

In areas where Gypsies had semi-permanent encampments - such as the Potteries in Notting Hill, London, or at Blackpool's South Shore - or in places where they returned annually for periods of several weeks for the harvesting of fruit or hop picking, you may find the children attended local schools, if only for short periods.

School registers can contain useful genealogical information about the child and its parents. They may also provide the date of the child's arrival in school, the date and reason for leaving and the destination the family was heading for. Some may also record which schools a child had attended previously which can assist in plotting the circuit the family had travelled.[34]

School records have generally been deposited in County Record Offices but occasionally remain with the schools themselves. A good starting point for checking what's available might be a search at the Access to Archives (A2A) site at www.nationalarchives.gov.uk/a2a

Indexes

General strays indexes

Most family history societies in Britain compile strays indexes. These can be a useful shortcut to the location of baptisms, marriages and burials of Gypsies on the move across county borders.

For the contact details of societies which belong to the Federation of Family History Societies, visit the Federation's website at www.ffhs.org.uk

The Federation itself holds a National Strays Index containing nearly 500,000 references. According to their website, this has recently been digitised in preparation for making it available online. For updates, check the FFHS Projects page at www.ffhs.org.uk

Specialist Gypsy indexes

• *Census entries website: http://members.shaw.ca/pauline777/TravellersUK.html*
A website compiled and hosted by Pauline Gashinski that contains references to showmen, fairground and circus Travellers and Gypsies, extracted principally from censuses and newspapers.

• *Romany Genes website: www.romanygenes.webeden.co.uk/*
Baptisms, marriages and burials extracted from parish registers and indexes.

• *Gypsies, Travellers and other Itinerants in Kent*
http://freepages.genealogy.rootsweb.ancestry.com/~gypsy/gypsy.htm
Baptisms, marriages, burials extracted from parish registers in Kent, plus newspaper items and pedlars' certificates from the Folkestone area.

• *Gypsies, Tramps and Strangers Volumes 1&2 and 3&4*
A collection of parish register and census entries compiled by Jenifer Edmonds and published on CD-ROM. Details (on receipt of an SAE) from Jenifer Edmonds, 51 Horns Lane, Norwich, Norfolk NR1 3ER, UK. E-mail: jenlibrary@aol.com Website: www.jenlibrary.u-net.com

• *Vagrants, Gypsies and Travellers in Kent*
Indexes of 16,000+ entries relating to baptisms, burials, Quarter and Petty Session appearances, settlements and removals gathered from Kentish sources. Details (on receipt of an SAE) from Gillian Rickard, 99 Strangers Lane, Canterbury, Kent CT1 3XN, UK, or from grickard@kentgen.com. Website: www.kentgen.com/vagrants.htm

• *Gypsies and the Law*
An index of references relating to Gypsies and Travellers caught up by the English legal system. This includes a large body of information on English Gypsies transported to the Americas and Australia between 1700 and 1868. Details (on

receipt of an SAE) from Sharon Floate, Beyond The Square, 75 Leonard Street, London EC2A 4QS, UK, or GypsyLawIndex@dsl.pipex.com

Single name studies for Gypsy surnames

A number of individuals are conducting studies of specific surnames and making their databases available to other searchers, for the most part online.

Black & White
http://black.and.white.tripod.com/welcome.htm

Brinkley
A one-name study on all Brinkleys but containing many references to travelling Brinkleys. Website: www.brinkleyfamily.co.uk

Draper
Contact: Sharon Floate, Beyond The Square, 75 Leonard Street, London EC2A 4QS, UK. E-mail: GypsyDraper@dsl.pipex.com

Loveridge & Smith
www.sarah-henson.co.uk/names/loveridge.htm

Scamp
Contact: Roger Baker, scamp@one-name.org

Specialist family history societies

Romany and Traveller Family History Society
The Romany and Traveller Family History Society was started in 1994 by a group of keen family historians with Gypsy/Traveller ancestors and continues to be the only family history society in Britain dedicated to this specialist interest. It has a worldwide membership, principally of people researching families in Britain. It is a member of the Federation of Family History Societies.

As well as publishing a quarterly journal - *Romany Routes* - containing features on sources, research tips, parish register and census finds, specific Gypsy family genealogies, customs and anecdotes, the Society holds open days and annual Society Days and has a mailing list exclusively for members. The Society Days include talks and presentations by leading authorities on Gypsy history, culture and genealogy and provide members and non-members with a forum for discussion and the sharing of experiences and knowledge. Back issues of *Romany Routes* are available to purchase.

The Society is also actively pursuing a publications policy and has produced a number of series of books relating to general Gypsy family history research, specific Gypsy family names, census extracts, oral history as related by present-day Travellers and aspects of Gypsy customs, culture and language. In addition, a series of important historical texts relating to the history of the Gypsies in Britain are being reprinted to make them accessible to a wider readership. A current publications list can be seen on the Society's website at www.rtfhs.org.uk . The Society also welcomes any Gypsy, Traveller and Fairground references found by researchers in historical documents. These can be sent to enquiries@rtfhs.org.uk

The Romani Association of Australia
Founded in 1990, the Association's aim is to assist people in Australia with Romani Gypsy ancestry in learning more about their culture and history. An important aspect of this is family history research and they have a Family History Adviser with extensive experience in this field to provide researchers with specialist help and advice.

The Society of Brushmakers' Descendants
Many Gypsies were involved in the making and hawking of brushes and brooms and may therefore be included in the records of this Society which specialises in brushmakers. Brushmaking was traditionally a 'travelling trade' even for its non-Gypsy exponents.

See the useful addresses section on p.107 for the contact details of these societies.

Gypsies in literature, art and photography

The colourful and exotic lifestyle of the Gypsies has made them a favourite subject for many writers of fiction and artists throughout history and in more recent times for photographers. A study of their works can provide the Gypsy family historian with an added bonus that is rarely available when searching for non-Gypsy ancestors of a similar class: pen-portraits of real people from the past captured in words and pictures.

One well-known example of an author with a particular passion for Gypsies is George Borrow (1803-1881). He wrote two semi-autobiographical novels - *Lavengro* (1851) and *The Romany Rye* (1857) - based on his encounters with the

Smith, Boswell/Boss, Herne and other Gypsy families he knew in East Anglia in the first half of the nineteenth century.

His character 'Jasper Petulengro' was the real-life Ambrose Smith (c1804-78) and his 'Flaming Tinman', one Riley Boswell or Boss. An outline of Ambrose Smith's family tree - as it was gathered from descendants of the family at the beginning of the twentieth century - was published in the *Journal of the Gypsy Lore Society* in January 1910 and is illustrated in the section on the *Journal* on p.72. The same article includes group photographs of some of these so-called 'Borrow's Gypsies', taken in Scotland in the late 1870s on the occasion of a visit to their camp by Queen Victoria. Many editions of Borrow's works include useful notes on the text which identify the 'fictional characters' by their real names.

The George Borrow Society was founded in 1991 to promote knowledge and research into the life and works of George Borrow. The Society publishes The George Borrow Bulletin twice a year and this often contains articles and items of interest to Gypsy family historians. A cumulative index for issues Nos. 1-20 is available and back issues can be purchased by non-members.

The author publishes a blog on the East Anglian Gypsy families who were known as 'Borrow's Gypsies': http://borrowsgypsies.wordpress.com

Charles Dickens (1812-1870) also made numerous references to Travellers in his works, not only as characters in his novels but also in the articles he wrote as a journalist. Many of these references have been collected by John Pateman and published in his *Charles Dickens and Travellers*.

A useful starting point for literary references to Gypsies is the anthology *The Wind on the Heath* by the Gypsiologist John Sampson (1863-1931). This gathers together extracts of writings about Gypsies from the time of Chaucer to about 1930 when the anthology was first published.

The artist Augustus John (1878-1961) - who was at one time President of the Gypsy Lore Society himself - was a regular visitor to the Gypsy encampments in and around Liverpool at the end of the nineteenth and beginning of the twentieth century. His paintings of Gypsies are mainly of those he encountered abroad but his biography by Michael Holroyd includes a number of useful references to the English Gypsy families John encountered in his travels in Britain. There is an Augustus John Archive in the National Library of Wales at Aberystwyth.

The artist Sir Alfred Munnings (1878-1959) made real-life Gypsies the subject of many of his fine paintings and drawings, some of which are now housed in the Sir Alfred Munnings Art Museum at Dedham near Colchester, Essex. He was a particularly close friend of the Gypsy Gray family of East Anglia and the Museum contains a fine early twentieth century portrait of Nellie Gray aka Bonnett, the daughter of Keomi Gray and Charles Bonnett. Munnings' autobiography includes accounts of the people he knew and his activities with them such as visits to fairs in Suffolk and further afield to the hop fields of Hampshire.

The Keomi Gray mentioned above was herself an artist's model. Before she became the partner of Charles Bonnett, Keomi had a relationship with the distinguished pre-Raphaelite artist Frederick Sandys (1829-1904) and had possibly three children by him who were raised as Gypsies. She was the subject of two of the most famous paintings of Sandys, his Medea (1868) and Morgan le Fay (1863-4).

Illustrations and photographs in the Journal of the Gypsy Lore Society

Throughout its history, the *Journal of the Gypsy Lore Society* regularly used engravings, woodcuts, paintings and photographs of Gypsies and Gypsy subjects to illustrate its articles, particularly in the issues published prior to the Second World War. Many of the originals of the photographs are now to be found in the Gypsy Collections of the University of Liverpool Library and in the Bodleian Library at Oxford University.

Of particular note in the Liverpool Collections are the magnificent photographs taken by Fred Shaw. These include many named portraits of Gypsies taken throughout England and Wales at the end of the nineteenth and the beginning of the twentieth century. Many have been used to illustrate the standard works on Gypsy life published since then. Samples can be seen here: http://sca.lib.liv.ac.uk/collections/colldescs/gypsy/photoind.htm

Family photographs

People with Gypsy and fairground ancestors are increasingly sharing the contents of their family photo albums with others, both online and in print. Because different families travelled and lived together, group shots can often include unrelated individuals with a variety of surnames, as well as the relatives of the photographs' owners. So it is always worth browsing the online portrait galleries and books on the off-chance that your own ancestors are included. *Romany Routes* - the quarterly journal of the Romany and Traveller Family History Society - includes photographs of this kind in every issue. For examples of what can be found in book-form, try *An RTFHS South Country Family Album* or Fred Price's *The Way of the Romany.* In both most individuals are named and locations are identified. Online the Romany Genes site at www.romanygenes.webeden.co.uk and the Romany Road site at www.romanyroad.co.uk include collections of photos contributed by individuals.

Picture postcards

A possibly overlooked source is picture postcards. Gypsies were a popular subject for postcards during the Edwardian era when this form of correspondence became something of a national craze in Britain. One example is shown on p.22.

In locations where there were semi-permanent encampments and where the Gypsies were something of a tourist attraction - such as Blackpool's South Shore - you may find series of postcards produced by enterprising local printers carrying named portraits or family groups.[35]

Robert Dawson's *A Directory of Gypsy Postcards* provides a comprehensive illustrated survey of postcards published in Britain, together with estimates of their modern-day market price. Gypsy postcards dating from the beginning of the twentieth century and modern reproductions of them are occasionally available for purchase from specialist booksellers: see the useful addresses section on p.107 for details.

REFERENCES

1. Fraser, Sir Angus, *The Gypsies*, p.69 (2nd. edn. Oxford, Blackwell, 1995)
2. Fraser, ibid, p.111
3. Fraser, ibid, p.112
4. Jarman, A O H and Eldra Jarman, *The Gypsies of Wales*, p.33 (Cardiff, University of Wales Press, 1991)
5. Jarman, ibid, p.5
6. Thompson, T W, 'The social polity of the English Gypsies', *Journal of the Gypsy Lore Society* 3rd Series vol. I pp.113-139 (Edinburgh, 1922)
7. Vesey-Fitzgerald, Brian, *Gypsies of Britain*, pp.55-6 (1st edn., Chapman & Hall, 1941)
8. Vesey-Fitzgerald, ibid, p.63
9. Vesey-Fitzgerald, ibid, p.57
10. Fraser, ibid, p.117
11. Winstedt, Eric Otto, 'Notes on English Gypsy Christian Names', *Journal of the Gypsy Lore Society* 3rd Series vol. I pp.65-90 (Edinburgh, 1922); 'Notes on English Gypsy Christian Names continued', *Journal of the Gypsy Lore Society* 3rd Series vol.II pp.16-39 (Edinburgh, 1923). See also Dawson, Robert, 'The name's NOT the same' *Romany Routes* vol. 1 no. 3 pp.95-97 (Romany and Traveller Family History Society, June 1995)
12. Okely, Judith, *The traveller-gypsies*, p.174 (Cambridge University Press, 1983)
13. Mayall, David, *Gypsy-travellers in nineteenth century society*, Chapter 3, pp.46-67 (Cambridge University Press, 1988)
14. Rickard, Gillian, *Vagrants, Gypsies and 'Travellers' in Kent 1572-1948*, p.56 (Canterbury, published by the author, 1995)
15. Floate, Sharon, *From welcome visitors to vagabonds: the history of the Gypsy encampment at South Shore, Blackpool 1840-1910*, Chapter 3, p.34 (University of London [Birkbeck College] Diploma thesis, 1993 - unpublished)
16. Death certificate of Elizabeth Robinson, 5 November 1895; baptised as Fabridge Smith, 14 November 1822, Great Holland, Essex
17. Keet-Black, Janet, 'So you've found Granny's baptism', *Romany Routes* vol. 2 no.3 pp.108-111 (Romany and Traveller Family History Society, June 1995)

18. Dawson, Robert, Yorkshire Gypsies, p.50 (Leyburn, N. Yorkshire, Bishopdale Archives, 1996)

19. Okely, ibid, p.226

20. Marsh, A E W, *A History of the Town and Borough of Calne*, p.163 (Calne, Wiltshire, Robert S Heath, 1904)

21. Vesey-Fitzgerald, ibid, pp.84-89

22. Smith, David, 'A seventeenth century tinker's will and inventory', *Journal of the Gypsy Lore Society* 4th Series vol.1 no.3 pp.172-177 (1977)

23. Hawkers' Licences 1697-99, The National Archives, London (TNA Ref. A03/370 and 371)

24. Boswell, Silvester Gordon, *The book of Boswell*, p.179 (Penguin Books, 1973)

25. Hawkes, Lt. Col. C P, 'Gypsy Blood', *Genealogists' Magazine* vol.6 no.9 p.395 (1934)

26. Lee, Terence, *The Smith Gypsy Genealogies and Related Families*, p.83 (Privately published by the author, 1995; new edition 2008)

27. Index of First World War Soldiers: Other Ranks, The National Archives, London (TNA Ref. WO 364). Also available online at www.nationalarchives.gov.uk/ documentsonline/medals.asp

28. Photograph collection of the author

29. Keet-Black, Janet, *The Sussex Gypsy Diaries 1898-1926* (Romany and Traveller Family History Society, 1999)

30. The Hall Papers, The Gypsy Collections, University of Liverpool (Ref. GLS/B5-8)

31. Mayall, ibid, Chapter 5, pp.97-129

32. 1851 census returns for Farnham, Dorset (TNA Ref. HO 107 1854 folio 68); see also Keet-Black, Janet, 'Stumpy Jack, pupil of the Farnham Gypsy School', *Romany Routes* vol. 1 no.2 pp.60-62 (Romany and Traveller Family History Society, March 1995)

33. McGowan, Alan, *On the Gypsy Trail: sources for the family historian*, p.23 (Romany and Traveller Family History Society, 1998)

34. Yates, Dora, 'An English Gypsy School', *Journal of the Gypsy Lore Society* 3rd Series vol.26 p.86 (1946)

35. Bennett, Peter, *Blackpool Pleasure Beach: a centenary of fun*, pp.27-28 (Blackpool Pleasure Beach, 1996)

APPENDIX ONE

Select calendar of legislation affecting Gypsies in England and Wales 1530-1910

1530 Egyptians Act
Accused *'outlandish People calling themselves Egipcions'* of fortune telling, deception, felony and robbery. Banned them from entering England and gave notice to those in England to leave the country within 16 days or to risk imprisonment and confiscation of their possessions.

1554 Egyptians Act
Forbade Gypsies from entering England and imposed the death penalty on those who remained in the country for more than a month.

1562 Egyptians Act
Extended the provisions of the previous Act to include *'counterfeit Egyptians'*: people who lived and travelled like Gypsies.

1596 Poor Law Act
Declared as rogues and vagabonds *'all tynkers wandering abroade...and all such p'sons, not being Felons, wandering and p'tending themselves to be Egipcians or wandering in the Habite Forme or Attyre of counterfayte Egipcians.'*

1597 Vagrancy Act
Made it possible for *'such as will not be reformed of their roguish kind of life'* to be conveyed to *'parts beyond the seas'.*

1656 Council of State order under Oliver Cromwell
Authorised *'the apprehending of lewd and dangerous persons who have no way of livelihood...and treating with merchants for transporting them to the English colonies in America'.*

1662 Settlement Act

Imposed controls on the free movement of every member of the population and offered a reward of 2 shillings for the apprehension of each beggar. Justices of the Peace were given powers to transport those deemed to be *'incorrigible rogues'*.

Act of 1697

Created a system of licensing for hawkers, pedlars and petty chapmen. The licence was to cost £4 per annum, plus an additional £4 if travelling with a horse, mule, ass or other beast bearing or drawing burden.

Acts of 1739-40 & 1743-4

Enabled Justices of the Peace to imprison in a House of Correction any rogue or vagabond. These included: persons pretending to be Gypsies or wandering in the habit of Egyptians, telling fortunes; petty chapmen and pedlars not licensed; all persons wandering abroad, lodging in alehouses, barns and outhouses and in the open air and not giving a good account of themselves.

1783 Egyptians Act

Repealed previous Acts against Gypsies, including the death penalty.

1783 Rogues and Vagabonds Act

Extended the provisions relating to the treatment of rogues and vagabonds.

1810 Hawkers and Pedlars Act

Consolidated a licensing system for hawkers and pedlars.

1822 Vagrancy Act

Consolidated and simplified previous acts relating to vagrants, rogues and vagabonds by repealing and then replacing most of their provisions.

1822 Turnpike Roads Act

Made Gypsies camping on the side of turnpike roads liable to a fine of 40 shillings.

1824 Vagrancy Act

Imposed a penalty of three months' imprisonment on those found pretending to tell fortunes by palmistry or other means and on anyone found wandering or lodging under a tent or cart who did not have any visible means of sustenance and not giving a good account of himself.

1835 Highways Act

Made Gypsies camping on the highway liable to a fine of 40 shillings.

1839 Reform of Constabulary Act
Established a national force of constables to police not only major towns and cities but rural areas also.

1876 Commons Act
Gave local authorities the power to pass bye-laws to close commons to Gypsies.

1885 Housing of the Working Classes Act
Extended the provisions of the Public Health Act of 1875 which covered the accommodation of hop pickers, to also encompass tents and vans.

1889 Infectious Diseases (Notification) Act
Encompassed both moveable dwellings and houses in its provisions relating to the control of diseases.

1889 Local Government Act
Enabled county councils to make bye-laws to control vagrancy.

1891 Public Health (London) Act
Imposed new sanitary regulations on vans and tents as well as houses.

1894 Local Government Act
Provided parish councils with the power to control the use of village greens and open spaces.

1899 Commons (Inclosure) Act
Enabled district councils to apply to the Board of Agriculture to make bye-laws controlling the use of commons.

1908 Children's Act
Made education compulsory for the children of Travellers.

Sources: David Mayall, *Gypsy-travellers in nineteenth-century society;* and Gillian Rickard, *Vagrants, Gypsies and 'Travellers' in Kent 1572-1948.*

APPENDIX TWO

Gypsy surnames and their distribution

This Appendix is provided as a general guide to the wide range of Gypsy surnames the family historian is likely to encounter and not as a definitive list. The area where a particular name is frequently found should also be taken purely as a starting point for research rather than as a geographical limit. In some cases, you will find the same name listed under two or more regional headings.

A more comprehensive list can be found in Robert Dawson's *Gypsy Names for Genealogists Volume 1: Surnames.*

Found throughout England

Boswell	Lee/Leigh/Lea	Taylor
Gray/Grey	Shaw/Shore	Young
Herne/Hearne/Heron/	Smith	(Heron often used as an alias)
Herring		
(Young often used as an alias)		

Northern England and Scottish Borders

Allen	Gaskin	Young
Blythe	Heron	(Heron often used as an alias)
Boswell	(Young often used as an alias)	
Faa/Faw	Winter	

Southern England

Ayers/Ayres/Eyres	Bowers	Coates
Ball	Brazil	Cole
Beeney/Beaney	Bunce	Cooper
Bird	Burton	Dennard

Doe	Keat/Keet	Ripley
Draper	Kemp	Rossiter
Francom/Frankham	Matthews	Saunders
Green	Miles	Scamp/Skemp
Gregory	Mills	Sherred
Hughes	Pateman	Stanley
Harris	Penfold/Pinfold	Vinden
Hawkins	(sometimes an alias for Palmer)	White
James	Pidgley/Pedgley	Williams
Johnson	Rawlings	

Eastern Counties

Boss	Gumble	Shaw
Boswell	Holland	Smith
Brown	Hope	Taylor
Chilcott	Lee	Thorpe
Deighton/Dighton	Nicholls/Nicholson	Webb
Gaskin	Penfold/Pinfold	West
Gray/Grey	Robinson	Whatnell/Watland

Central England

Bagley	Draper	Peace/Pearce/Pierce
Biddle	Lovell	Scarrett/Scarrott
Buckland	Loveridge	Smith
Buckley	McLean/Macklin	Welch/Welsh
Clayton	Marshall	

Western England

| Brinkley | Orchard | Small |
| Camfield | Penfold/Pinfold | Stephens/Stevens |

Wales and Welsh Borders

Bridges	Jones	Price
Davies	Lee	Roberts
Evans	Lock/e	Williams
Florence	(sometimes an alias for	Wood
Griffiths	Boswell)	
Ingram	Lovell	

BIBLIOGRAPHY

Bennett, Peter, *Blackpool Pleasure Beach: a centenary of fun* (Blackpool Pleasure Beach, 1996).

Binns, Dennis, *A gypsy bibliography* (Manchester, Dennis Binns Publications, 1982; supplements 1986, 1988).

Black, George, *A Gypsy Bibliography* (1st edn. 1914; reprinted Michigan, USA, Gryphon Books, 1971).

Boswell, Silvester Gordon, *The book of Boswell: autobiography of a Gypsy* (Penguin Books, 1973).

Borrow, George, *Lavengro* (1st edn. 1851).

Borrow, George, *The Romany Rye* (1st edn. 1857).

Bridgeman, Ian and Clive Emsley, *A guide to the archives of the Police Forces of England and Wales* (Police History Society, 1992).

Cameron, David Kerr, *The English Fair*, (Stroud, Sutton Publishing, 1998).

Christian, Peter and Annal, David, *Census: The Expert Guide* (The National Archives, 2008).

Churchill, Else, *Census copies and indexes in the Library of the Society of Genealogists* (3rd edn. Society of Genealogists, 1997).

Coldham, Peter Wilson, *The Complete Book of Emigrants in Bondage 1614-1775* (Baltimore, USA, Genealogical Publishing Co. Inc., 1988) Also available on CD-ROM together with The Complete Book of Emigrants 1607-1776 (same publisher, 1996).

Cole, Anne, *An Introduction to Poor Law Documents before 1834* (Federation of Family History Societies, 2nd edn. 2000).

Dawson, Robert, *A Directory of Gypsy Postcards* (2nd edn. Alfreton, published by the author, 1999).

Dawson, Robert, *Gypsy Names for Genealogists Volume 1: Surnames* (Alfreton, published by the author, 2000).

Dawson, Robert, *Gypsy Names for Genealogists Volume 2: Forenames* (Alfreton, published by the author, 2000).

Floate, Sharon, *From welcome visitors to vagabonds: the history of the Gypsy encampment at South Shore, Blackpool 1840-1910* (University of London [Birkbeck College] Diploma thesis, 1993 - unpublished).

Fraser, Sir Angus, *The Gypsies* (2nd edn. Oxford, Blackwell, 1995).

Garner, Ken and Jack Parker, *Hertfordshire Settlement Certificates* (Hertfordshire Family & Population History Society, 2001).

Gibson, Jeremy, *Bishops' Transcripts and Marriage Licences* (2nd edn. Birmingham, Federation of Family History Societies, 1982).

Gibson, Jeremy, *Marriage and Census Indexes for family historians* (Birmingham, Federation of Family History Societies, 1998).

Gibson, Jeremy, *Militia Lists and Musters 1757-1876* (3rd edn. Birmingham, Federation of Family History Societies, 1994).

Gibson, Jeremy, *Quarter Sessions Records for family historians* (Birmingham, Federation of Family History Societies, 1995).

Gibson, Jeremy and Colin Rogers, *Poor Law Union Records* (Birmingham, Federation of Family History Societies, 1993).

Gibson, Jeremy and Elizabeth Hampson, *Specialist Indexes for family historians* (Birmingham, Federation of Family History Societies, 1998).

Griffin, Ken, *Transported beyond the Seas: an alphabetical listing of criminals. prosecuted in Hertfordshire who received transportation sentences to Australia 1784-1866* (Hertfordshire Family & Population History Society, 1997).

Hawkings, David, *Bound for Australia* (Chichester, Phillimore, 1987).

Hawkings, David, *Criminal Ancestors* (Stroud, Alan Sutton, 1992).

Hearn, John, *John's Story* (Romany and Traveller Family History Society, 2001).

Holroyd, Michael, *Augustus John: the new biography* (Chatto & Windus, 1996).

Holt, the Reverend T E, *Travelling Folk: Itinerant Mission in the Diocese of Salisbury, 1882-1883*. Transcribed for publication by Rosemary Church (Wiltshire Family History Society, 1999).

Jarman A O H and Eldra Jarman, *The Gypsies of Wales: the children of Abram Wood* (Cardiff, University of Wales Press, 1991).

Journal of the Gypsy Lore Society, 1888-1973.

Keet-Black, Janet, *Some Travellers in the 1891 Census Volumes 1-4* (Romany and Traveller Family History Society, 1999-2002).

Keet-Black, Janet, *The Sussex Gypsy Diaries 1898-1926* (Romany and Traveller Family History Society, 1999).

Lee, Terence, *The Smith Gypsy Genealogies and Related Families* (Privately published by the author, 1995; new edition 2008).

Lewis, Pat, *My ancestor was a Freemason* (Society of Genealogists, 1999).

Lincolnshire County Council, *Convicts of Lincolnshire* (Lincolnshire County Council, 1988).

Lincolnshire Family History Society, *Lincolnshire Poor Law Indexes* (various years) .

Logan, Roger, *An Introduction to Friendly Society Records* (Federation of Family History Societies, 2000).

Loveridge, Pat, *A Calendar of Fairs and Markets held in the nineteenth century* (Romany and Traveller Family History Society, 2003).

Marsh, A E W, *A History of the Town and Borough of Calne* (Calne, Wiltshire, Robert S Heath, 1904).

Mayall, David, *Gypsy-travellers in nineteenth century society* (Cambridge University Press, 1988).

McGowan, Alan, *On the Gypsy Trail: sources for the family history of Gypsies* (Romany and Traveller Family History Society, 1998).

McGrigor Phillips, Dorothy, *The Romany Collection, University of Leeds* (Edinburgh, Thomas Nelson, 1962).

Munnings, Sir Alfred, *An Artist's Life* (Museum Press, 1950).

Munnings, Sir Alfred, *The Finish* (Museum Press, 1952).

Newington-Irving, Nicholas, *Will indexes and other Probate Material in the Library of the Society of Genealogists* (Society of Genealogists, 1996)

Okely, Judith, *The traveller-gypsies* (Cambridge University Press, 1983).

Owen's New Book of Roads being a Companion to Owen's Book of Fairs (Scratcherd and Letterman, 1817).

Pateman, John, *Seven Steps to Glory: Private Pateman Goes to War* (Romany and Traveller Family History Society, 2002).

Register of Pedlars Certificates of the City of Exeter, 1871-1874 (Devon Family History Society, 2003).

Rickard, Gillian, *Vagrants, Gypsies and 'Travellers' in Kent 1572-1948* (Canterbury, published by the author, 1995).

Romany Routes, journal of the Romany and Traveller Family History Society, (December 1994-present).

Russell, Alexander, *Index to the Old Series of the Journal of the Gypsy Lore Society 1888-1892* (Edinburgh, T & A Constable, 1914).

Sampson, John, *The Wind on the Heath* (Chatto & Windus, 1930).

Scott Macfie, Robert, *A catalogue of gypsy books collected by Robert Scott Macfie* (Liverpool, University of Liverpool, 1937).

Spencer, William *Army Records: A Guide for Family Historians* (The National Archives, 2008).

Spencer, William *First World War Army Service Records: A Guide for Family Historians* (The National Archives, 2008).

Starsmore, Ian, *English Fairs* (Thames & Hudson, 1975)

Swinstead, J H, *Parish on Wheels* (1st edn.1897; reprinted by the Wiltshire Family History Society, 1999).

Tate, W E, *The Parish Chest* (Chichester, Phillimore, 1983)

Vesey-Fitzgerald, Brian, *Gypsies of Britain: an introduction to their history* (1st edn. Chapman & Hall, 1944).

BACKGROUND READING

Publications on specific Gypsy surnames

Ayres/Ayers

Booth

Trudgill, Eric, *The Family Trees of Francis and Mary Clayton & John and Mary Booth from about 1750 to about 1900, from the South Midlands of England to the North East and North West* (Romany and Traveller Family History Society, 2009).

Bowers

McGowan, Alan, *On the Gypsy Trail: sources for the family history of Gypsies* (Romany and Traveller Family History Society, 1998).

Boswell

Boswell, Silvester Gordon, *The book of Boswell: autobiography of a Gypsy* (Penguin Books, 1973).

Buckland and Buckley

Hayward, Jim, *Travellers & Fairkeepers from the Cotswolds & Vale of White Horse to Regions Beyond Part 1: The Buckland Family, their kith and kin* (Carterton, Oxfordshire, privately published by the author, 2000. Contact: Jim Hayward, Carterton Breeding Aviaries, Brize Norton Road, Carterton, Oxfordshire OX18 3HW, UK. e-mail: hayward@ witneyserve.net).

Hayward, Jim, *Travellers & Fairkeepers from the Cotswolds & Vale of White Horse to Regions Beyond Part 2: Abraham Buckland and His Children* (Carterton, privately published by the author, 2000).

Hayward, Jim, *Travellers & Fairkeepers from the Cotswolds & Vale of White Horse to Regions Beyond Part 3: Mantus Buckland, His Kin and Their Associates* (Carterton, privately published by the author, 2001).

Ing, Leonard, *Index of Buckland and Buckley names extracted from the Journal of the Gypsy Lore Society 1888-1973* (Romany and Traveller Family History Society, 1997).

Dawson, Robert, *The Genealogy of the Romany Boswells Volume 1: The Pedigrees* (Romany and Traveller Family History Society, 2004).

Dawson, Robert, editor, *Henry Dry-Bread: The Richard Wade Papers* (Alfreton, published by the author, 2000).

Clayton

Trudgill, Eric: see Booth above.

Elliott

Halton, Vivienne M, *The Descendants of John and Jemima Elliott and Related Families* (Romany and Traveller Family History Society, 2010).

Harris

Page, Ken, *The Story of Harris's Fun Fairs - Eastern Counties, Midlands and Beyond* (Privately published by the author, 1998).

Hearn

Trudgill, Eric, *The Family Trees of Benjamin and Thomas Hearn from about 1740 to about 1900, mainly counties to the north, west and south of London* (Romany and Traveller Family History Society, 2009).

Lee

Lee, Terence, *The Lee Family Tree: the Lee and Smith Gypsies Volume 1* (Privately published by the author, 1992; new edition 2008).

Lee, Terence, *The Lee Family Tree: the Lee and Smith Genealogies Volume 2* (Privately published by the author, 1993; new edition 2008).

Trudgill, Eric, *The Family Trees of Damon and Thomas Lee from about 1750 to about 1900 mainly the English southern counties* (Romany and Traveller Family History Society, 2008).

Loveridge

Loveridge, Pat, *The Family Tree of William and Margaret Loveridge from about 1750 to about 1900 mainly Northamptonshire and nearby counties* (Romany and Traveller Family History Society, 2008).

Manning

Haines, H.J. *Mannings Amusements: Chronicle of a Hertfordshire Family* (Halstead Press, Essex, 1989).

Matthews

Brown, Frances, *Fairfield Folk* (1st edn. Malvern, Malvern Publishing Company, 1986).

Pateman

Pateman, John, *Hoo, Hops and Hods: the life and times of Robert Pateman.*

(The Pateran Press, Lincoln, 2008 - full text available online at Google Books: http://books.google.com).

Pateman, John, *Strewing the Pateran: the Gypsies of Thorney Hill* (The Pateran Press, Lincoln, 2008 - available to purchase as a downloadable book or a printed book at Lulu: www.lulu.com).

Roberts

Jarman, A O H and Eldra Jarman, *The Gypsies of Wales: the children of Abram Wood* (Cardiff, University of Wales Press, 1991).

Scamp

Baker, Roger, *The Family Tree of Samson and Celia Scamp from about 1750 to about 1900 mainly Kent and nearby counties* (Romany and Traveller Family History Society, 2008).

Shaw

Page, Ken: see Harris above.

Smith

Hayward, Jim, *Travellers & Fairkeepers from the Cotswolds & Vale of White Horse to Regions Beyond Part 4: Alabon Smith and Some of His Tribe, with Addenda and Revisions to Parts 1, 2 and 3* (Carterton, privately published by the author, 2001).

Lee, Terence: see Lee above.

Lee, Terence, *The Smith Gypsy Genealogies and Related Families* (Privately published by the author, 1995; new edition 2008).

Smith, Cornelius, *The Life History of Gypsy Cornelius Smith* (1st edn. John Heywood, 1890; reprinted by the Romany and Traveller Family History Society with introduction, biographical notes and census returns by Sharon Floate, 2000).

Smith, George 'Lazzy', *Incidents in a gipsy's life: the Royal Epping Forest Gipsies* (1st edn. Liverpool, International Exhibition, Liverpool 1886; reprinted by the Romany and Traveller Family History Society with introduction, biographical notes and census returns by Sharon Floate, 2001).

Smith, Rodney, *Gypsy Smith, His Life and Work by Himself* (National Council of Evangelical Free Churches, 1902).

Tombs, Josephine, *The Family Tree of Woodfine Smith from about 1750 to about 1900, mainly the English Midlands and North West* (Romany and Traveller Family History Society, 2009)

Spurrett

Hayward, Jim, *Travellers & Fairkeepers from the Cotswolds & Vale of White Horse to Regions Beyond Part 5: The Spurretts, Their Families & Associates* (Carterton, privately published by the author, 2002).

Welch

Page, Ken: see Harris above.

Wood

Jarman, A O H and Eldra Jarman: see Roberts.

Sampson, John, *The Dialect of the Gypsies of Wales* (Oxford, Clarendon Press, 1926).

Wood, Manfri, *In the Life of a Romany Gypsy* (Routledge, 1979).

General publications listing Gypsy surnames and forenames

Dawson, Robert, *Gypsy Names for Genealogists Volume 1: Surnames* (Alfreton, published by the author, 2000).

Dawson, Robert, *Gypsy Names for Genealogists Volume 2: Forenames* (Alfreton, published by the author, 2000).

Dawson, Robert, *Romany Forenames: Comparisons of Four Major Families - Boswell, Heron, Lee, Smith* (Romany and Traveller Family History Society, 2004).

Register of Traveller Research: surname interests of members of the Romany and Traveller Family History Society (Romany and Traveller Family History Society, 1995).

Register of Traveller Research: Supplement 1 (Romany and Traveller Family History Society, 1997).

Publications on the general histories of Gypsies in specific counties or regions

Hampshire

Cuttriss, Frank, *Romany Life - Experienced & Observed During Many Years of Friendly Intercourse with the Gypsies* (Mills & Boon, 1915)

Smith, Len, *Romany Nevi-Wesh: An Informal History of the New Forest Gypsies* (Nova Foresta, 2004).

Kent

Evans, Simon, *Stopping Places - A Gypsy History of South London and Kent* (University of Hertfordshire Press, 2004).

Warwickshire

Rudge, Ted, *Brumroamin: Birmingham and Midland Romany Gypsy and Traveller Culture* (Birmingham, Birmingham Library and Information Service, 2003).

West Country - Devon, Cornwall and Somerset

Levinson, Martin and Silk, Avril, *Dreams of the Road - Gypsy Life in the West Country* (Birlinn, 2007).

Yorkshire

Dawson, Robert, *Yorkshire Romanies* (Leyburn, N. Yorkshire, Bishopsdale Archives, 1996).

Saunders, Peter and others, *Gypsies and Travellers in their own words - words and pictures of travelling life* (Leeds Traveller Education Publishing Group, 2000).

Romani language

Acton, Thomas and Donald Kenrick, *Romani Rokkeripen to-divvus* (Brentwood, Essex, Romanestan Publications, 1984).

Borrow, George, *Romano Lavo-Lil* (1st edn. 1874; reprinted Stroud, Alan Sutton, 1982; available online as an electronic book at http://onlinebooks.library.upenn.edu/ webbin/gutbook/lookup?num=2733).

Coughlan, Tim, *Now Shoon the Romano Gillie: Traditional Verse in the High and Low Speech of the Gypsies of Britain* (Cardiff, University of Wales Press, 2001).

Dawson, Robert, editor, *Henry Dry-Bread: The Richard Wade Papers* (Alfreton, published by the author, 2000) (contains an Anglo-Romani vocabulary).

Dawson, Robert, *The Dialect of Derbyshire Traditional Travellers* (Alfreton, published by the author, 2002).

Hayward, James, *Gypsy Jib: A Romany Dictionary* (Wenhaston, Holm Oak Publishing, 2003).

McGowan, Alan, *The Winchester Confessions 1615-1616* (Romany and Traveller Family History Society, 1996).

Sampson, John, *The Dialect of the Gypsies of Wales* (Oxford, Clarendon Press, 1926).

Smart, Bath and Henry Crofton, *The Dialect of the English Gypsies* (Asher & Co., 1875).

Texts including genealogical information on Gypsy families

Carew, Francis Wylde (alias A E Way), *No. 747: being the autobiography of a gipsy* (J W Arrowsmith, 1891).

Chandler, Keith, *Gypsies, Hawkers and Other Travellers in the English South Midlands* (Romany and Traveller Family History Society, 2005).

Chandler, Keith, *More Gypsies, Hawkers and Other Travellers in the English South Midlands & Including East Anglia, The Home Counties & The South East* (Romany and Traveller Family History Society, 2007).

Davies, Jennifer, *Tales of the Old Gypsies* (Newton Abbot, David & Charles, 1999).

Groome, Francis Hindes, *In gipsy tents* (1st edn. 1880; reprinted Wakefield, EP Publishing, 1973).

Hall, the Reverend George, *The gypsy's parson* (Sampson Low & Co., 1915; full text available online at www.archive.org/details/gypsysparsonhise00hallrich).

Morwood, Vernon S, *Our gypsies in city, van and tent* (Sampson Low Marston Searle and Rivington, 1885).

Rudge, Ted, *Brumroamin: Birmingham and Midland Romany Gypsy and Traveller Culture* (Birmingham, Birmingham Library and Information Service, 2003).

Yates, Dora, *My Gypsy Days* (Phoenix House, 1953).

Gypsy culture and lifestyle

Harvey, Denis, *The gypsies: waggon-time and after* (Batsford, 1979).

Holt, the Reverend T E, *Travelling Folk: Itinerant Mission in the Diocese of Salisbury, 1882-1883*. Transcribed for publication by Rosemary Church (Wiltshire Family History Society, 1999).

Ingram, Peter and John Barker, *Romany Relics: The Wagon Album* (2010: details from www.romanyrelics.com)

Jones, E Alan, *Yorkshire Gypsy fairs, customs and caravans* (Beverley, Yorkshire, Hutton Press, 1986).

Kenrick, Donald, *Gypsies: from the Ganges to the Thames* (An extended new edition of the book originally published in 1993 as *Gypsies: from India to the Mediterranean*) (Hatfield, University of Hertfordshire Press, 2004).

Lee, Ken, 'Australia - Sanctuary or Cemetery for Romanies?', *Romani culture and Gypsy identity*, edited by Acton, Thomas, and Gary Mundy (Hatfield, University of Hertfordshire Press, 1997).

Mayall, David, *English Gypsies and State Policies* (The Interface Collection: Hatfield, University of Hertfordshire Press, 1995).

Sandford, Jeremy, *Gypsies* (Abacus, 1975).

Ribton Turner, C J, *A History of Vagrants and Vagrancy* (Chapman and Hall, 1887).

Stanley, Betsy, *Memories of the Marsh: A Traveller Life in Kent* (Romany and Traveller Family History Society, 1998).

Swinstead, J H, *Parish on Wheels* (1st edn.1897; reprinted by the Wiltshire Family History Society, 1999).

Thorburn, Gordon and J Baxter, *The Appleby Rai: travelling people on a thousand year journey* (Appleby, Cumbria, Fido, 1996).

Travellers Remember Hopping Time (Romany and Traveller Family History Society, 2003)

Ward-Jackson, C and Denis Harvey, *The English gypsy caravan* (Newton Abbot, Devon, David and Charles, 1986).

USEFUL ADDRESSES

Specialist archives

UK

The Gypsy Collections, Sydney Jones Library, University of Liverpool, PO Box 123, Liverpool L69 3DA, UK.
- E-mail: k.hooper@liv.ac.uk
- Website: http://sca.lib.liv.ac.uk/collections/colldescs/gypsy/index.htm

The Romany Collection, Brotherton Library, University of Leeds, Leeds LS2 9JT, UK.
- E-mail: library@leeds.ac.uk
- Website: www.leeds.ac.uk/library/spcoll/virtualtour/side_romany.htm

The Robert Dawson Romany Collection, Museum of English Rural Life, University of Reading, Redlands Road, Reading, Berkshire RG1 5EX, UK.
- E-mail: merl@reading.ac.uk
- Website: www.reading.ac.uk/merl

Bodleian Library, Oxford University Library Services, Broad Street, Oxford, Oxfordshire OX1 3BG, UK.
- Website: www.ouls.ox.ac.uk/bodley

USA

The Romani Archives and Documentation Center, Calhoun Hall 501, The University of Texas B5100, Austin, TX 78712, USA.
- Website: www.radoc.net

Victor Weybright Archives of Gypsy Studies, The Gypsy Lore Society, 5607 Greenleaf Road, Cheverly, Maryland 20785, USA.
- Website: www.gypsyloresociety.org

Museums with Gypsy collections

The Gordon Boswell Romany Museum, Clay Lake, Spalding, Lincolnshire PE12 6BL, UK.
* Website: www.boswell-romany-museum.com

The Museum of East Anglian Life, Stowmarket, Suffolk IP14 1DL, UK
* Website: www.eastanglianlife.org.uk

The South East Romany Museum, Twin Oaks, Howlands Lane, Marden, Kent TN12 9LB, UK.
* Website: www.southeastromanymuseum.co.uk/index.htm

Photographic collections

The Gordon Boswell Romany Museum, Clay Lake, Spalding, Lincolnshire PE12 6BL, UK.
* Website: www.boswell-romany-museum.com

The Gypsy Collections, University of Liverpool - see Specialist archives

Bodleian Library, University of Oxford - see Specialist archives

New Forest Museum, New Forest Centre, Lyndhurst, Hampshire SO43 7NY. Holds the Jack Loveland collection of photographs of New Forest Gypsies taken in the 1950s and 1960s.
* Website: www.newforestmuseum.org.uk

Online photographic collections

The Borrow's Gypsies Blog: photographs and articles relating to the East Anglian Gypsy families who were known to George Borrow.
* Website: http://borrowsgypsies.wordpress.com

The Living Album - Hampshire's Gypsy Heritage: online collection
* Website: www.hants.gov.uk/rh/gypsy/resources.art.htm

Passing Places - Hertfordshire's Gypsy Heritage: online collection
* Website: www.passingplaces.org.uk

Romany Genes - family photographs
* Website: www.romanygenes.webeden.co.uk

Romany Road - family photographs
* Website: www.romanyroad.co.uk

Romany Wales Project - the Gypsies of Wales: online collection
* Website: www.valleystream.co.uk/romhome.htm

Family history societies

Romany and Traveller Family History Society, c/o Sharon Floate, Beyond The Square, 75 Leonard Street, London EC2A 4QS, UK.
- E-mail: enquiries@rtfhs.org.uk
- Website: www.rtfhs.org.uk

Society of Brushmakers' Descendants, 13 Ashworth Place, Church Langley, Essex CM17 9PU, UK.
- E-mail: s.b.d@lineone.net
- Website: www.brushmakers.com

Romani Association of Australia Inc, 9 Corrigin Heights, Parmelia, WA 6167, Australia.

Fairground and circus information

National Fairground Archive, Western Bank Library, University of Sheffield, Sheffield S10 2TN, UK.
- E-mail: nfa@sheffield.ac.uk.
- Website: www.nfa.dept.shef.ac.uk

Fairground Association of Great Britain: Membership Secretary, 29 Mill Street, Belper, Derbyshire DE56 1DT, UK.
- Website: www.fagb.co.uk

The Fairground Society: Simon Harris, The Membership Secretary, PO Box 549, Tweedale, Telford TF7 5WA, UK.
- Website: www.fairgroundsociety.co.uk

The Fairground Heritage Trust and Centre, Milford, Lifton, Devon PL16 0AT, UK
- Website: www.fairground-heritage.org.uk

Discussion forums on fairground and circus ancestors:
- Website: www.fairground-heritage.org.uk/forum/

Circus Friends Association:
- Website: www.circusfriends.co.uk
- E-mail: cfa-secretary@aol.com

World's Fair (newspaper publisher), 3rd Floor, Hollinwood Business Centre, Albert Street, Oldham, Lancashire OL8 3QL, UK.
- E-mail: info@worldsfair.co.uk
- Website: www.worldsfair.co.uk

Legal records

Quarter Sessions records - online name searches

A2A (Access to Archives)
- Website: www.nationalarchives.gov.uk/a2a

The Old Bailey Session Papers - online index
- Website: www.oldbaileyonline.org

Police Forces Archives. *A Guide to the Archives of the Police Forces of England and Wales,* published 1992 by Bridgeman and Emsley, is now available online
- Website: www.open.uk/arts/history/policing/police-archives-guide/index.html

Organisations for the preservation and promotion of Gypsy culture

The Gypsy Council for Education, Culture, Welfare and Civil Rights, European and UK Office, 8 Hall Road, Aveley, Essex RM15 4HD, UK.
- Website: www.thegypsycouncil.org.uk

Romani Association of Australia Inc., 9 Corrigin Heights, Parmelia, WA 6167, Australia.

Gypsy Lore Society, 5607 Greenleaf Road, Cheverly, Maryland 20785, USA.
- Website: www.gypsyloresociety.org

Specialist booksellers and publishers

Cottage Books, Gelsmoor, Coleorton, Leicestershire LE67 8HR, UK.
- E-mail: jenny@friendlyweb.co.uk

Robert Dawson, 188 Alfreton Road, Blackwell, Alfreton, Derbyshire DE55 5JH, UK.
- E-mail: bob@robertdawson.co.uk. Website: www.robertdawson.co.uk

Graham York, 225 High Street, Honiton, Devon EX14 1LB, UK.
- E-mail: books@gyork.co.uk. Website: www.gyork.co.uk

Romanestan Publications, 22 Northend, Worley, Brentwood, Essex CM14 5LA, UK.
- E-mail: T.A.Acton@greenwich.ac.uk

University of Hertfordshire Press, College Lane, Hatfield, Hertfordshire AL10 9AB, UK.
- E-mail: uhpress@herts.ac.uk.
- Website: www.herts.ac.uk - and search by 'Romani Studies' on the home page

Freemasons and friendly society archives

The United Grand Lodge of England, Freemasons Hall, 60 Great Queen Street, London WC2B 5AZ, UK.
- Website: www.ugle.org.uk
- E-mail for genealogical enquiries: libmus@ugle.org.uk

Royal Antediluvian Order of Buffaloes, Grand Lodge of England, Grove House, Skipton Road, Harrogate, Yorkshire HG1 4LA, UK.
- Website: www.raobgle.org.uk
- E-mail: hq@raobgle.org.uk

National Register of Archives: for locating friendly society registers
- Website: www.nra.nationalarchives.gov.uk/nra

Gypsies in literature and art

The George Borrow Society. Membership information: M. K. Skillman, 60 Upper Marsh Road, Warminster, Wiltshire BA12 9PN, UK.

- Website: www.clough5.fsnet.co.uk/gb.html

Art galleries

The Sir Alfred Munnings Art Museum, Castle House, Dedham, Colchester, Essex CO7 6AZ, UK.
- Website: www.siralfredmunnings.co.uk

Specialist mailing lists/message boards

Travelling People. A message board for those with Romany Gypsy, Traveller, Fairground and Circus ancestors. An archive of messages can be browsed at the site.
- www.rootschat.com/forum/index.php/board,387.0.html

UK-Romani-L. For those with a genealogical interest in Gypsies in the UK. An archive of mailings can also be consulted. Information from:
- http://lists.rootsweb.ancestry.com/index/other/Ethnic-Romani/UK-ROMANI.html

Romany Routes. A mailing list exclusively for members of the Romany and Traveller Family History Society. Information from:
- www.rtfhs.org.uk - and select Romany Routes E-mail List from the menu.

Aus-Romani-L. For those with a genealogical interest in Gypsies in Australia. The site has an archive of mailings that can be browsed. Information from:
- http://lists.rootsweb.ancestry.com/index/intl/AUS/AUS-ROMANI.html

Online search tools

Sites that provide useful links to sources on the history of Gypsies/Travellers:

Cyndi's List. Gypsy, Romani, Romany & Travellers pages.
- Website: www.CyndisList.com/peoples.htm#Gypsies

The Gypsy Collections, University of Liverpool.
- Website: http://sca.lib.liv.ac.uk/collections/colldescs/gypsy/index.htm

Romany and Traveller Family History Society
- Website: www.rtfhs.org.uk

Travelling People Message Board
- Website: www.rootschat.com/forum/index.php/board,387.0.html

GLOSSARY

A glossary of Romani words and other special terms used in the text

Anglo-Romani   the form of Romani spoken by Gypsies in England and Wales.

atchin tan   camping or stopping place.

dukkering   fortune telling.

Egyptian   Gypsy.

gaujo   non-Gypsy (can also be spelt 'gorger').

mulo   spirit, ghost.

petulengro   horseshoe maker, the Romani word for the surname 'Smith'.

Romani   the language of the Gypsies (can also be spelt 'Romany').

Romanichal   the Anglo-Romani term used by Gypsies to describe themselves.

vardo   caravan.

INDEX

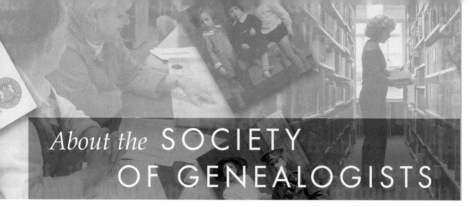

www.sog.org.uk

Founded in 1911 the Society of Genealogists (SoG) is Britain's premier family history organisation. The Society maintains a splendid genealogical library and education centre in Clerkenwell.

The Society's collections are particularly valuable for research before the start of civil registration of births marriages and deaths in 1837 but there is plenty for the beginner too. Anyone starting their family history can book free help sessions in the open community access area where assistance can be given in searching online census indexes or looking for entries in birth, death and marriage indexes.

The Library contains Britain's largest collection of parish register copies, indexes and transcripts and many nonconformist registers. Most cover the period from the sixteenth century to 1837. Along with registers, the library holds local histories, copies of churchyard gravestone inscriptions, poll books, trade directories, census indexes and a wealth of information about the parishes where our ancestors lived.

Unique indexes include Boyd's Marriage Index with more than 7 million names compiled from 4300 churches between 1538-1837 and the Bernau Index with references to 4.5 million names in Chancery and other court proceedings. Also available are indexes of wills and marriage licences, and of apprentices and masters (1710-1774). Over the years the Society has rescued and made available records discarded by government departments and institutions but of great interest to family historians. These include records from the Bank of England, Trinity House and information on Teachers and Civil Servants.

Boyd's and other unique databases are published on line on **www.origins.com**, on **www.findmypast.com** and on the Society's own website **www.sog.org.uk**. There is free access to these and many other genealogical sites within the Library's Internet suite.

The Society is the ideal place to discover if a family history has already been researched with its huge collection of unique manuscript notes, extensive collections of past research and printed and unpublished family histories. If you expect to be carrying out family history research in the British Isles then membership is very worthwhile although non-members can use the library for a small search fee.

The Society of Genealogists is an educational charity. It holds study days, lectures, tutorials and evening classes and speakers from the Society regularly speak to groups around the country. The SoG runs workshops demonstrating computer programs of use to family historians. A diary of events and booking forms are available from the Society on 020 7553 3290 or on the website **www.sog.org.uk** .

Members enjoy free access to the Library, certain borrowing rights, free copies of the quarterly *Genealogists Magazine* and various discounts of publications, courses, postal searches along with free access to data on the members' area of our website and each quarter to our data on **www.origins.com**.

More details about the Society can be found on its extensive website at **www.sog.org.uk**

For a free Membership Pack contact the Society at:

14 Charterhouse Buildings,
Goswell Road,
London EC1M 7BA
Telephone 020 7553 3291
Fax 020 7250 1800

The Society is always happy to help with enquiries and the following contacts may be of assistance.

Library & shop hours:

Monday	Closed
Tuesday	10am - 6pm
Wednesday	10am - 6pm
Thursday	10am - 8pm
Friday	Closed
Saturday	10am - 6pm
Sunday	Closed

Contacts:

Membership
Tel: 020 7553 3291
Email: membership@sog.org.uk

Lectures & courses
Tel: 020 7553 3290
Email: events@sog.org.uk

Family history advice line
Tel: 020 7490 8911
See website for availability